HEALTH CARE
and the RISE *of*
CHRISTIANITY

D1564018

HEALTH CARE
and the RISE *of*
CHRISTIANITY

HECTOR AVALOS

HENDRICKSON
PUBLISHERS

© 1999 Hector Avalos
Hendrickson Publishers, Inc.
P. O. Box 3473
Peabody, Massachusetts 01961–3473

Printed in the United States of America

ISBN 1–56563–337–7

First Printing — September 1999

Library of Congress Cataloging-in-Publication Data

Avalos, Hector.
    Health care and the rise of Christianity / Hector Avalos.
    Includes bibliographical references and index.
    ISBN 1–56563–337–7 (pbk.)
    1. Healing—Religious aspects—Christianity—History of
doctrines—Early church, ca. 30–600. 2. Healing—Religious
aspects—History of doctrines. 3. Healing—Rome—History.
I. Title.
BT732.2.A93   1999
261.8'321'09015—dc21   99–11023
                                                            CIP

On the cover: Christ healing the blind man. Byzantine Collection,
Dumbarton Oaks, Washington, D.C.

Table of Contents

Abbreviations

General

ca.   circa
NRSV   New Revised Standard Version

Dead Sea Scrolls

CD   *Damascus Document*
4QMMT   *Miqsat Maʿaseh ha-Torah*
11QTemple *Temple Scroll*

Talmud and Related Literature

y. Ber.   *Berakot* (Jerusalem)
t. Ḥul.   *Tosefta Ḥullin*

Other

T.   Testimonia and sources concerning Asclepius, as
           numbered and edited in Ludwig Edelstein and Emma
           Edelstein, *Asclepius*. 2 vols. Baltimore, 1945.

Modern Publications

AJA   *American Journal of Archaeology*
AMT   *Assyrian Medical Texts*. R. C. Thompson. Oxford,
           1923
ANF   *Ante-Nicene Fathers*
ANRW   *Aufstieg und Niedergang der römischen Welt: Geschichte
           und Kultur Roms im Spiegel der neueren Forschung*. Ed.
           H. Temporini, W. Haase. Berlin, 1972–

AnSt	*Anatolian Studies*
BA	*Biblical Archaeologist*
BAR	*Biblical Archeology Review*
BR	*Biblical Research*
BRev	*Bible Review*
BTB	*Biblical Theology Bulletin*
CBQ	*Catholic Biblical Quarterly*
CQ	*Classical Quarterly*
DJD	Discoveries in the Judaean Desert
DSST	*The Dead Sea Scrolls Translated: The Qumran Texts in English.* Florentino García Martinez. Leiden, 1994
EPRO	Études preliminaires aux religions orientales dans l'empire romain
Frayne	Douglas R. Frayne. *The Royal Inscriptions of Mesopotamia: Old Babylonian Period (2003–1595 BC).* RIME 4. Toronto, 1990.
HSM	Harvard Semitic Monographs
HTR	*Harvard Theological Review*
IEJ	*Israel Exploration Journal*
JAOS	*Journal of the American Oriental Society*
JBL	*Journal of Biblical Literature*
JJS	*Journal of Jewish Studies*
JNES	*Journal of Near Eastern Studies*
JRS	*Journal of Roman Studies*
LABS	*Letters from Assyrian and Babylonian Scholars.* Ed. Simo Parpola. Helsinki, 1993.
LCL	Loeb Classical Library
NTS	*New Testament Studies*
OEANE	*The Oxford Encyclopedia of Archaeology in the Near East.* Ed. E. M. Meyers. New York, 1997.
Or	*Orientalia* (New Series)
PGM	*Papyri graecae magicae: Die griechische Zauberpapyri.* Ed. K. Preisendanz. Berlin, 1928.
RevQ	*Revue de Qumran*
RIME	Royal Inscriptions of Mesopotamia, Early Periods
SecCen	*Second Century* (see *Journal of Early Christian Studies*)
TS	Texts and Studies
TZ	*Theologische Zeitschrift*
ZPE	*Zeitschrift für Papyrologie und Epigraphik*

Foreword

This book represents the marriage of the two fields in which I was formally trained, anthropology and biblical studies. I hope that I have done justice to them both. This book also represents a continuation of the interest in health care systems reflected in my previous book, *Illness and Health Care in the Ancient Near East*, which focused on pre-Christian periods.

Whenever it is feasible, I provide the reader with the full passage in the original language of most classical sources quoted in English. Because of their accessibility, biblical texts in their original languages are not provided unless specific words or phrases are at issue. Because of the difficulty in reproducing all of the sigla in *Miqsat Maᶜaseh ha-Torah* (4QMMT), I do not provide the Hebrew for this source.

I am greatly indebted to Adam Meseke, Lisa Morse, Shana Wilson, and Cassie Wyant, who, as research assistants at Iowa State University, helped to gather library materials and/or proofread various versions of this book. As always, I am the most grateful to my wife, who has suffered countless days of watching her husband fixated on a computer screen.

Introduction

María Atkinson (1879–1963) was a Mexican woman who had been raised a Catholic.[1] Her biographer reports that one day in 1924 she walked out of her doctor's office with a diagnosis of cancer. Her Catholic faith was apparently not providing a satisfactory cure. The search for a cure took her to various towns in the American Southwest, including El Paso, Phoenix, and Tucson, but she could not find relief.

After spending nearly all of her assets on doctors, she finally decided to follow the advice of two female acquaintances who belonged to a Pentecostal group, which, besides believing in the imminent return of Christ, emphasized healing. They had a very simple prescription: prayer and anointing with oil. So they anointed her with oil and prayed for her. Soon, it is reported, she became better. This experience convinced Atkinson that she must leave Catholicism and join Pentecostalism.

María Atkinson eventually became the founder of the Church of God in Mexico. Beginning with only Atkinson in 1931, the Mexican branch of the Church of God, a Pentecostal denomination with world headquarters in Cleveland, Tennessee, in 1993 reported about 53,000 members in Mexico alone. Her efforts in founding the Church of God in Mexico are one reason María Rivera Atkinson is called the "mother of Mexico" by many of her admirers.

María Atkinson exemplifies what has been a recurrent theme in many religions. Converts often are initially attracted to a new group because of practical health care concerns. Even though the Church of God was very eschatologically oriented, it was not the theology of the end of the world that first attracted Atkinson to found this group. Rather, it was the practical concern of restoring her health. Atkinson had, in effect, decided to become part of a new health care system represented by Pentecostalism. She became a great advertiser for the Pentecostal way of healing, not only in her sermons but also in the banner she hung at the altar with the slogan in Spanish: "Jesús sana" ("Jesus heals").

The paradox was, however, that Atkinson remained sickly all of her life despite her belief in Pentecostal faith healing. Given that neither conventional medicine nor Pentecostalism provided the desired results, we must explain her attraction and conversion to Pentecostalism by considering a wider array of benefits that the Pentecostal health care system provided her. For example, if neither conventional physicians nor Pentecostalism heal, at least Pentecostalism does not charge for its services. If neither conventional health care nor Pentecostalism can cure cancer, at least Pentecostals can provide a simplified health care strategy that eliminates the sometimes complex travel to various clinics and institutions required by conventional health care.

Although the advent of the kingdom of God is a prominent theme in the New Testament, it is clear that health is portrayed as one of the most persistent practical concerns of those who eventually converted to Christianity. Many of the stories in the Gospels portray converts as initially seeking not some eschatological kingdom but, rather, simple healing. Thus the woman (Mark 5:25–34) who touches Jesus' garment is not portrayed as seeking the kingdom of God; rather, she wants healing. The centurion in Luke 7:1–10 does not ask first about the kingdom of God; rather, he wants Jesus to heal his servant. The parent of the demon-possessed youth (Mark 9:14–29//Luke 9:37–43) does not come to Jesus because he is interested in eschatology; rather, he is interested in curing his son. And Paul, the foremost of the apostles, says in Gal 4:13, "You know that it was because of a physical infirmity that I first announced the gospel to you."[2] Regardless of the historicity of this claim in Galatians, Luke agrees that Paul came to Ananias in Damascus as a blind man (Acts 9:18–19).

It is, indeed, difficult to ignore the numerous healings that are attributed to Jesus in the New Testament. According to some counts, there are about forty-one healings ascribed to Jesus in the Gospels.[3] Health care, then, should not be seen as just a literary topos or excuse to showcase Jesus' power in the New Testament. Healing may not just be a sign of the arrival of the kingdom of God. Health care, far from being a peripheral service, can be the core of a new religious movement. Thus, healing can be the principal factor in attracting new converts who are desperate to relieve themselves of one of the most universal of human problems—illness.

BRIEF STATEMENT OF THE THESIS

The ideas of health care reflected in early Christianity constitute a system that was an important factor in attracting converts. As such, these ideas about health care constitute an important factor in the rise of Christianity itself. It is true that the themes of salvation and eschatology were important and affected the way in which many stories about illness were constructed. It is also true that literary motives also played a role in healing narratives.[4] The thesis here, however, is that the role of health care in the rise of Christianity has not been given as much credit as it is due.

The distinctive aspects of Christian health care may be seen when we compare it with the health care systems offered by other Greco-Roman religious and secular traditions as well as the health care system evinced in Leviticus. Despite the diversity of Judaism, the book of Leviticus remained perhaps the most influential scriptural authority on health care in most forms of Judaism in the first and second centuries. While many individual components of the Christian health care system may also be found in the other health care systems of the Greco-Roman world, Christianity, despite its diversity, had a configuration of health care options and ideas that conferred many advantages for many patients.

Although it is reasonable to believe that Jesus probably did engage in healing activities, this study does not focus on proving that the historical Jesus performed the particular healings attributed to him. Rather, it focuses on how healing was portrayed and promoted by the community responsible for the New Testament and other early Christian literature. We focus on how people in the first and second centuries might have viewed the advantages of the messages of healing reflected in early Christian literature in light of other systems of health care to which they were exposed in the ancient Mediterranean world.

Likewise, this thesis does not depend on showing that Christian healings were real while those of other religions were not. We cannot establish historically or scientifically that Christianity had any advantage in the efficacy of its miracles or healings relative to other religions or secular traditions. Indeed, it is assumed here that the efficacy of Christianity's medical or miraculous treatments was no better than the efficacy of any other religion. The point is that, all ancient religions being relatively equal in the efficacy of claimed healing miracles, any advantage offered by Christianity resided in a constellation of other features of its health care system.

A HEALTH CARE CRISIS IN THE FIRST CENTURY?

The introduction of new religious traditions correlates with health care crises at various times in the ancient world. For example, Asclepius was introduced into Athens after a plague in 429 B.C.E. Likewise, the cult of Asclepius was introduced into Rome in 291 B.C.E. after a plague.[5] Some temples of Isis, the Egyptian goddess of healing, were built in order to ensure the health of emperors, such as Hadrian.[6]

Despite the occurrence of well-known plagues in the centuries prior to the rise of Christianity, the first and second centuries probably brought a relatively higher incidence of disease. One reason was the rapid urbanization in the first century.[7] It is well known that epidemics require certain thresholds in population densities in order to thrive.[8] William H. McNeill, the famed historian of epidemics in history, notes that measles "requires a population with at least 7,000 susceptible individuals perpetually in its ranks. . . . The critical threshold below which the virus cannot survive falls between 300,000 and 400,000 persons."[9]

Many of the principal cities where Christianity first appeared experienced large population surges in the first century. Rome approached perhaps a million people by the end of the reign of Augustus.[10] Not surprisingly, an epidemic in Rome in 65 C.E. killed perhaps some thirty thousand persons.[11] Roman Corinth, which began with a few thousand colonists in 44 B.C.E., had swelled to perhaps a hundred thousand inhabitants by the beginning of the second century.[12] Likewise, Ephesus increased in population during the first century, numbering perhaps a hundred thousand by the beginning of the second century. The relevance of Ephesus's growth for the New Testament is stated by L. Michael White: "The urban growth shifted gears smoothly after the *damnatio memoria* of Domitian and developed rapidly under Trajan and Hadrian. It is also worth noting that this is the same period during which Acts was probably written and Christianity grew in Ephesus."[13] Indeed, these large population surges would have been apparent to New Testament writers.

The increasing population density would also have increased the opportunity for illness caused by malnutrition. Indeed, malnutrition was perhaps a constant cause of disease in cities with large populations.[14] Herod the Great exerted great effort ameliorating a famine that occurred in Judea in 28/27 B.C.E.[15] One physician reports that rickets, a disease associated with malnutrition, was quite common among children in the second century.[16] It may be no accident that, in the first century, Pliny the Elder speaks of the appearance of new diseases in Rome, most notably disfiguring skin diseases that may also be associated with malnutrition.[17]

The rise of the army formed a massive vector of disease as soldiers traveled to and from the East. Many of the most serious plagues began among troops, who brought many of these epidemics into large cities and into their own hometowns. One of the best examples is the plague attributed to Roman troops returning from the Near East to the western portion of the Roman Empire in the second century. This plague raged for fifteen years and claimed the lives of perhaps five thousand persons in Rome alone, including the emperor Marcus Aurelius Antoninus, who wrote about the pestilence in his celebrated *Meditations*.[18]

Christianity, therefore, may have arisen at a time when concerns about illness were entering even more into the consciousness of people because of the rise of urbanization, travel, and other important factors that increase susceptibility to diseases. This again indicates that the frequency of illness reports in the New Testament may not simply serve literary purposes. Even if the prominence of healing is not due to some sort of crisis during the first century, such narratives reflect very practical concerns that are universal—illness and health care.

JESUS' HEALINGS IN SCHOLARSHIP

For much of this century, research into the historical Jesus by biblical scholars has minimized the role of healing in Jesus' activities. Thus Stevan Davies notes that "the paradigm of Jesus the Healer is practically unheard of in Historical Jesus studies."[19] The role of miracle and healing has been obscured by the emphasis on salvation history and eschatology in the agendas of modern scholarship. For example, in *The New Testament and Its Modern Interpreters*, a standard compendium on the current status of the field of New Testament studies, there is not a single heading devoted to health care or Jesus' activity within a health care system.[20]

The minimization of healing as an important part of early Christianity has been echoed even by some scholars working outside biblical studies. Darrel Amundsen, in his recent wide-ranging history of medicine, states,

> Although the New Testament emphasizes the miracles of Jesus and, to a lesser extent, those of the apostles as substantiating proofs of the truth of Christianity, the role of healing miracles within the Christian community and as part of the evangelistic enterprise during the second and third centuries was so minor as to be nearly negligible.[21]

Amundsen's claim is based on an article by Gary Ferngren in a prestigious journal.[22] Such assertions have been countered by Vivian Nutton, another eminent historian of medicine, who has also noted Christian competition with other religions in healing miracles.[23] The lack of a response to Ferngren by New Testament scholars betrays the lack of dialogue between New Testament scholars and historians of medicine.

At the same time, recent historical-Jesus "questers" agree that the historical Jesus was probably engaged in healing activities. Such scholars include John Dominic Crossan, who describes the strategy of his reconstructed Jesus as "a combination of *free healing* and *common eating,* a religious and economic egalitarianism that negated alike and at once the hierarchical and patronal normalcies of Jewish religion and power."[24] Likewise, John Meier, in his massive study of the historical Jesus, decries those who previously suppressed the notion of Jesus as healer. One of his conclusions is that the best historical criteria indicate that "Jesus performed certain actions during his public ministry that both he and some of his contemporaries thought were miraculous healings of the sick or infirm."[25]

If we value the criterion of embarrassment to determine the activities of the historical Jesus, then Mark 6:5 probably reaches back to an authentic tradition about Jesus: "And he could do no deed of power there, except that he laid his hands on a few sick people and cured them."[26] Such an admission by a pro-Jesus writer would not be likely unless there was a reliable and undeniable tradition that Jesus actually had attempted to work healing miracles, albeit his inefficacy was blamed on unbelief.

In sum, there are indications of a reaction against the dominance of studies of the historical Jesus that had deemphasized the role of healing in early Christianity. Rodney Stark, though not focusing on health care, also recently shows that socioeconomic factors merit more attention in explaining the rise of Christianity.[27] What has been lacking in New Testament scholarship is a systematic comparison of the socioeconomic advantages that Christianity offered in its health care system to those offered by other religions and secular medical traditions in the Mediterranean basin.

PREVIOUS TRADITIONAL RESEARCH

This inquiry applies new perspectives from medical anthropology, which focuses on the study of health care as a human institution. The idea that health care forms a system is a crucial feature of medical anthropology. In large part, the purpose of this study is to explain how the findings of anthropologists concerning health care systems may be applied to the study of the rise of Christianity. "Traditional research" here refers to studies that do not integrate in a systematic manner the findings of modern medical anthropology with critical biblical studies. Since medical anthropology is a relatively new field, virtually all studies of health care prior to the 1980s may be seen as traditional.

One early advocate of the idea that health care was an important factor in the rise of Christianity was Adolf von Harnack:[28] "Christianity is a medical religion: that is its strength and, in many aspects, also its weakness."[29] He acknowledged that Christian ideas about healing were in significant competition with Greco-Roman traditions. His observations were never developed systematically, however, and he lacked the data that medical anthropologists now have collected regarding the behavior of patients in health care systems. Harnack's focus was on an attempt to explain the success of Christianity rather than on a systematic comparison between Christianity and contemporary religions.

Many subsequent scholars alluded to competition between Christian and non-Christian health care, but again such observations were not developed systematically.[30] Bernd Kollmann is perhaps the scholar who has best developed the observations of Harnack.[31] He also notes the economic advantages of Christian medicine and provides an excellent comparative discussion. Nonetheless, he does not see health care as a system, nor is he much interested in medical anthropology. Dieter Lührmann still appears correct in his observation: "Such a brief and necessarily cursory survey of the study of New Testament miracle stories shows that the comparison with ancient medicine has heretofore played no role."[32]

Other scholars have engaged in historical study of Christian healing in order to make the case that Christianity has abandoned and should restore an emphasis on healing. For example, Evelyn Frost's main contribution was *Christian Healing*, a collection and analysis of statements in the ante-Nicene fathers concerning healing.[33] But she never systematically compared non-Christian traditions with which Christianity might have been in competition.

Morton Kelsey makes a similar plea for restoring healing ministries in *Healing and Christianity*, which also includes a historical analysis of healing in Christianity. He sees many parallels between the techniques of Jesus and those of Carl Jung, the famed Swiss psychologist. Indeed, Kelsey advocates a Jungian approach to modern healing in general. Kelsey notes that eliminating illness was an important part of early Christianity but that theological developments, dating particularly from the time of Pope Gregory I, shifted the emphasis to illness as something to be endured rather than eliminated.[34]

Kelsey addresses non-Christian traditions in a cursory manner, however, and some of his pronouncements are often too general or inaccurate. He often accepts without much criticism the historicity of healing stories. Kelsey's notion of a health care system is tied to the basic ideas of illness and healing, rather than to broader concerns of patients.

NEW APPROACHES IN NEW TESTAMENT STUDIES

Sociological and anthropological approaches to the New Testament are no longer a novelty, but medical anthropology still is in its infancy insofar as New Testament studies are concerned.[35] Most biblical scholars still have little formal training in anthropology, and even less in medical anthropology. Still, some noteworthy studies of early Christian health care attempt to integrate ideas from medical anthropology. Most studies are usually short, however, and the notion of health care as a system still lacks a full-length study.

One example of such studies is a series of articles written by John Pilch. He is one of the first scholars to apply the notion of health care as a system to the New Testament, although his focus is not on a systematic comparison of the early Christian health care systems with those of non-Christian traditions.[36] Pilch's most valuable contribution is to bring some medical anthropological models to the attention of New Testament scholarship.[37]

On the other hand, Pilch exemplifies a common problem: attempting an interdisciplinary approach without the benefit of formal training in the relevant disciplines. Indeed, there is sometimes a tendency to apply to biblical studies the models of anthropologists thought to be paradigmatic, without paying attention to dissenting viewpoints within the anthropological community.

As shown below, Pilch relies excessively on the models of Mary Douglas to explain early Christian health practices. Douglas's model, for all its useful application in biblical studies, has significant limitations, especially in explaining purity laws and illness.[38] I disagree with Pilch's proposal that the "state of being," rather than the function of an individual in society, best explains the notion of purity and illness in the ancient Mediterranean world. In the model presented here, function and "state of being" are inextricably complementary and not mutually exclusive categories (see below).

The focus on Jesus as a healer has been prominent in the work of Morton Smith.[39] Smith argues that Jesus' activities were not principally modeled on Israelite prophets but, rather, on magicians of the Hellenistic world; exorcisms, for example, were not found among the Israelite prophets but were common among Greco-Roman magicians. The raising of the dead performed by Jesus resembles more the work of Apollonius of Tyana, the famous first-century healer, than that of prophets such as Elijah or Elisha.

Smith's celebrated study, *Jesus the Magician,* precipitated much discussion. His critics have argued that he used inappropriate parallels—for example, Apollonius, the principal narratives about whom are products of the third century.[40] Nonetheless, Smith made a valuable contribution by placing Jesus and early Christianity within a wide spectrum of "magical" practices in the Mediterranean world.

Howard Clark Kee's 1986 study of health care in early Christianity, *Medicine, Miracle, and Magic in New Testament Times,* is perhaps the most important in the last two decades.[41] He includes extensive discussions of various Greco-Roman traditions. But as the title of his book suggests, Kee was principally preoccupied with the relationship of Christianity to the "three major modes of healing— medicine, miracle, and magic—which are in competition with each other in this period."[42] For Kee, Christianity was distinguished by its selection of miracle as the primary mode of healing. Accordingly, he does not compare systematically the components of health care systems but, rather, alludes to such components (e.g., economics) as they pertain to his main typology. He also does not delve deeply into other contemporary religious traditions; for example, Isis is discussed in a few paragraphs.[43] We shall review later the usefulness of Kee's typology.

In *Jesus the Exorcist*, Graham Twelftree considers healing as a central aspect of Jesus' ministry, but Twelftree's purpose is not to compare the health care systems of the first century. Rather, he provides a portrayal of Jesus' self-understanding of his healing ministry and discusses how this healing ministry was understood by his contemporaries and followers. Twelftree concludes that Jesus is best seen as an exorcist, and he summarizes the role of exorcism as follows: "However, while exorcism was by no means the only aspect of his ministry, particularly in his exorcisms (carried out by the power-authority of the eschatological Spirit) he believed the first stage in the defeat of Satan and his kingdom was taking place in order that the kingdom of God could come."[44] Twelftree represents a worthy attempt to correct the expulsion of healing from the ministry of the historical Jesus, while retaining the eschatological importance of his healing ministry.[45]

In *Jesus the Healer*, Stevan Davies portrays Jesus as part of a movement that saw possession as a defining characteristic: "The foundational event of the Christian religion was the mass spirit-possession of Jesus' followers (just as Jesus' own initial possession experience, at his Baptism, was the foundational event of his career)."[46] Despite his appeal to anthropological studies, Davies does not intend to provide a systematic comparison of health care systems. Instead, he employs cross-cultural studies in order to show that Jesus, as a healer who stressed spirit possession, used altered states of consciousness in his healing activities: "It is predictable and likely that Jesus made use of altered states of consciousness among his healed and exorcised associates in the process of effecting their full cure."[47] Some of Davies's ideas may seem questionable, and he ignores the work of Pilch. Still, Davis makes a strong case that spirit possession played a far greater role in Christian theology, at least as portrayed by the New Testament authors, than most New Testament scholars admit.

One final example is Harold Remus's *Jesus As Healer*.[48] Despite his earlier work comparing Christian and Hellenistic concepts on magic, Remus exemplifies how little medical anthropology has penetrated New Testament studies. Remus still seems content with summarizing Jesus' healing activities on a book-by-book basis. He is not interested in any systematic attempts to compare various health care systems of the Mediterranean world.

In summary, some of the newer approaches to healing in the New Testament use sociological and anthropological materials, but they still lack a thorough comparative approach based on the perspective of health care as a system.

CURRENT DEBATES AND THE PRESENT THESIS

A number of developments that have occurred in the last two decades in the study of Judaism and Greco-Roman civilizations provide new opportunities for the study of health care in early Christianity. For example, a new edition of Galen's *On Physicians*, which survives only in Arabic, bears important information about the status of physicians and the options available to patients.[49] New demographic data and mortality studies from ancient Rome help us explore how the seasonal variations in mortality affected the use of healing resources by patients.[50]

At the same time, there are debates that encourage a critical reexamination of some of the assumptions and conclusions of previous studies involving health care issues. In particular, the notion of a unified Judaism in the first century is increasingly under question. The idea, most often associated with George Foot Moore, that there was a normative Judaism has steadily yielded to studies that show a wide diversity in almost every aspect of Judaism.[51] Some of the well-known divisions of first-century Jews into Sadducees, Pharisees, and Essenes are no longer seen as very clear.[52] The uncertainty about Jewish sectarianism in the first century is aligned with the increasing reluctance to equate situations described in rabbinic literature with those found in the first century.[53]

Such caution regarding the use of rabbinic literature is particularly important in light of the recent publication of *Miqsat Maʿaseh ha-Torah* (Some precepts of the Torah), an important manuscript from the Dead Sea caves.[54] The basic contents of this document, better known as 4QMMT, were made public in 1984, though allusions to it date back to the early days of Dead Sea Scrolls research. *Miqsat Ma'aseh ha-Torah* contains various comments on purity and on the differences between the authors of this document and what is apparently the temple establishment of Jerusalem. Daniel Schwartz believes that the document neutralizes the positions of Morton Smith and Jacob Neusner, who argued that rabbinic Judaism was not to be equated with the Pharisaic positions.[55] Nonetheless, *Miqsat Ma'aseh ha-Torah* helps to confirm that the purity laws pertaining to certain illnesses mentioned in Leviticus and elsewhere in the Hebrew Bible were indeed taken seriously during at least part of the late Second Temple period.[56]

The association of the Dead Sea Scrolls with the Essenes has become particularly problematic. Once, virtually all Dead Sea Scrolls scholars subscribed to the theory that the scrolls in the Dead Sea caves were produced by the Essenes, who are said to have inhabited the nearby ruins called Qumran.[57] Now a number of important scholars question whether (1) the Dead Sea Scrolls were primarily the product of the Essenes;[58] (2) Qumran has any necessary or proven relationship to the scrolls in the caves; (3) all or any of the scrolls derived from a single sect, Essene or not; and (4) Qumran was the home of any sort of Jewish group or sect at all.[59] The recent publication, by F. M. Cross and Esther Eshel, of an ostracon that supposedly would decide the matter in favor of the Essene hypothesis has only aroused more debate.[60]

Some scholars also question, to some extent, whether we can speak of monotheism in Judaism.[61] The difficulty in speaking of monotheism in the Judaism of late antiquity is foregrounded by the new publication of Jewish amulets, some of which were not considered in previous major discussions concerning health, magic, and other related theological ideas. As Joseph Naveh and Shaul Shaked, two of the foremost specialists on these amulets, note, "The most conspicuous objective for which the amulets in our collection have been prepared is to address health problems."[62] Such texts may help illuminate the role of magic and syncretism in health care options available in the Near East.

Archaeological research has brought to light new materials from Galilee.[63] The relationship of the area's culture to that of Jerusalem is becoming better known. One of the most prominent issues arising out of these explorations is the extent to which Galilee was hellenized. Eric Meyers, for example, argues against Crossan and other scholars who see Jesus' Galilean homeland as extensively hellenized.[64] Others argue that no extensive hellenization is needed to explain any postulated assimilation of the ideas of the Cynics by Jesus in Galilee.

This discussion should prompt us to proceed with caution as well as optimism in the study of health care systems in the first and second centuries. This study does not depend on rabbinic texts to develop its arguments, nor does its thesis claim to identify the specific positions of Jewish sects. It does claim that certain health practices advocated by the Jewish group that became known as Christianity differed from those of other Jewish groups, regardless of whether we attach the rubric of Pharisee, Sadducee, or Essene to those groups.

This study remains agnostic about the equation between the Essenes and the community or communities that produced the Dead Sea Scrolls. Even if the scrolls cannot be firmly identified with the Essenes, these materials certainly reflect concepts that were important to at least some Jewish communities of the first century. In sum, despite the limits discussed above, there is sufficient information to establish the thesis.

LITERARY-CRITICAL METHODOLOGY

This study cannot recapitulate the entire history of scholarship on various issues pertaining to the New Testament and early Christianity, and choices are inevitable when we are confronted with major disagreements in New Testament scholarship. Specific controversial issues will be discussed in the relevant portions of the study. For the moment, I shall briefly note some of its major assumptions and methods.

The complex nature of the Gospels, in particular, is beyond the scope of a detailed examination here. The claims of this inquiry do not always require isolating the earliest strands of a particular tradition, for it is not claiming that all healing ideas can be traced back to the historical Jesus or even the earliest strands of the Christian tradition. The *completed* Gospels and other New Testament books, however, do reflect a distinctive combination of Christian solutions to problems that occurred in health care in the first and second centuries.

In many cases, however, a plausible case can be made that such solutions or health practices reflect an early Christian tradition that may reach back to the historical Jesus. In such cases, I follow the majority of modern scholars in accepting the two-source hypothesis as the most useful for analyzing the traditions behind the Gospels.[65] I shall defend such an analysis only when relevant.

Many healing stories, in their current canonical form, were meant to illustrate broader theological agendas about eschatology or the arrival of the kingdom of God. This study will also argue, however, that many New Testament writers evince clear concerns with promoting the advantages of Christian health care in the face of the health care practices found in traditional Jewish and Greco-Roman traditions.

HISTORICAL AND GEOGRAPHICAL LIMITS

The focus here is on the first century C.E. for obvious reasons: Jesus and Paul, the primary founders of Christianity, lived in the first century, and most of the New Testament was composed in that century. The first century B.C.E., on the other hand, is crucial for highlighting the developments just prior to the rise of Christianity that rendered the latter distinctive.[66]

This essay's significant interest in the second and third centuries provides an opportunity to see whether some of the ideas concerning health care expressed in the New Testament writings continued into these centuries in a coherent manner. In addition, it examines writers of the second and third centuries to see whether they saw such New Testament ideas as advantageous over other health care systems. This also allows the opportunity to see whether Christian health practices had any attraction for non-Christians. We are fortunate to have statements concerning health care from, among second- and third-century authors, Irenaeus (ca. 130–202), Justin Martyr (ca. 100–160), Origen (ca. 185–284), Tertullian (ca. 160–220), and Galen (ca. 129–216), the Roman physician.

The geographical focus is on the eastern Mediterranean, where Christianity developed. Aside from the obvious geographical range reflected in New Testament writings, many of the other health care traditions used here for comparison (e.g., those associated with Asclepius, Isis, and Hippocrates) were known throughout this area.

At the same time, since there was not always a homogeneous environment for every aspect of health care, regional differences, which should be appreciated, will be mentioned where appropriate.

SUMMARY

Despite some of the caveats engendered by recent studies of Judaism, the Dead Sea Scrolls, and the canonical Christian sources, there is sufficient information to establish that early Christianity evinced a system of health care that attracted many converts. Practical socioeconomics played as much of a role as religious factors in the rise of Christianity. The socioeconomic advantages of Christianity's health care system may be discerned by a consideration of specific aspects of the health care systems of the various religious and secular traditions with which Christianity was in competition.

CHAPTER ONE

Health Care As a System

The distinct approach of this study is drawn from recent advances in medical anthropology. In its most general sense, an anthropological approach to biblical studies seeks to apply the insights and theories that develop from the observation of actual societies.[1] Such insights may help place an ancient culture in perspective.

Foremost among the advances in medical anthropology is the exploration of health care as a system.

> The single most important concept for the cross-cultural studies of medicine is a radical appreciation that in all societies health care activities are more or less interrelated. Therefore, they need to be studied in a holistic manner as socially organized responses to disease that constitute a special cultural system: the *health care system*.[2]

A health care system may be defined as a set of interacting resources, institutions, and strategies that are intended to maintain or restore health in a particular community.[3] A health care system usually includes, but is not limited to, the presuppositions regarding the causes and diagnoses of illness, the options available to the patient, and the modes of therapy. Other dimensions include social or geographic differences in the accessibility to what is perceived to be the best care available in the society, and the society's attitudes toward the patient and the health care expert. Most health care systems, modern or not, offer a plurality of options for patients.

What a system intends is not always what it yields. Many systems aimed at preventing and curing illness[4] may have actually unintentionally promoted illness. For example, Asclepieia, which were meant to cure the sick, may have unintentionally caused the spread of illness in the larger community by concentrating large numbers of sick people in small places. Thus visitors who came to be cured of illness A at the Asclepieion may have contracted illness B from other patients at the temple. Illness B may have then been transported back to their homes.

In any event, since health care is being treated as a system, we must explore data from areas that might be relevant. These areas include ecology, demography, and paleopathology. Changes in the components or their relationships in a health care system may cause significant changes in the delivery of health care in a society.

Among the medical anthropologists to whom we are most indebted is Kleinman. In a series of articles and monographs and through extensive fieldwork, he has advanced the theoretical and practical aspects of medical anthropology.[5] Kleinman's is not the only approach that may be used in the study of health in the eastern Mediterranean at the time of Christianity's infancy. Nor can all aspects of his theories be applied in biblical studies. For the purposes here, one of the most crucial aspects of his approach is the focus on patients' strategies seeking health care. And among the important questions posed by Kleinman's approach are these: What options are available to the patient? Is there a hierarchy of options?

Historians of ancient medicine such as Mirko Grmek,[6] Nutton,[7] and Henry Sigerist[8] have provided many basic discussions of Greco-Roman medicine. And even if not all of his conclusions are acceptable, McNeill has integrated the study of history, demography, and health crises in a provocative manner.[9]

THE SOCIORELIGIOUS FRAMEWORK
OF A HEALTH CARE SYSTEM

In contrast to modern Western medicine, religion and health care were intricately intertwined in most of the ancient world. The religious framework of a culture is of utmost importance in determining the type of health care that a culture develops. Such influence, however, is not unidirectional. Health care needs also help to shape religious frameworks. At the most basic level, the number of gods in a religious system affects a health care system in a fundamental manner. Here we may distinguish two basic systems: polytheism and monolatry.

Polytheism, as a religious system that acknowledges the existence and/or legitimacy of many gods, affects a health care system in various ways. On the one hand, polytheism tends to provide patients with a number of divine options. If one deity does not afford an answer, the patient may go to another deity. Thus, polytheism offers more options for patients.

On the other hand, a polytheistic system can also complicate and render cumbersome the options available to a patient. Healing rituals, for example, may become long and elaborate because of the sheer number of gods that must be entreated or repelled. One example may be seen in a ritual against the disease identified as "malaria" by Simo Parpola, an Assyriologist.[10] In order to perform this ritual, one needed

> a figurine of the daughter of Anu (the primary sky god)
> a figurine of Namtar (a minor god of the underworld)
> a figurine of Latarak (a little-known figure)
> a figurine of Death
> a substitute figurine made of clay
> a substitute figurine made of wax
> . . . 15 drinking tubes of silver for Gula (goddess of healing) and Bēlet-ṣēri (mistress of the desert)
> . . . 7 twigs] of tamarisk
> 7 twigs of date palm
> [7 bot]tles of wine
> 7 bottles of beer
> [7 bottles] of milk
> 7 bottles of honey

The figurines of the deities, which were probably assembled in the presence of the patient or in some sacred area, represent the supernatural beings that needed to be appeased. The foods were probably intended as offerings to gain the favor of these deities. Prayers to the deities were probably combined with medical treatments applied to the patient, and the entire ritual might have lasted hours or even been spread over a few days. This catalog of items for the ritual against malaria illustrates that labor-intensive rituals were related, in large part, to the number of supernatural beings that were to be contacted, appeased, or repelled. The consultant often had to spend much time performing complicated rituals and procuring paraphernalia for different gods, even if a single illness was the object of the ritual.

The fact that such labor-intensive rituals affected the immediate availability of some health care consultants is also evident in the letter in which a king, probably Esarhaddon (681–669 B.C.E.), orders Marduk-šakin-šumi, an *āšipu* (the term for one of the main healing consultants of Mesopotamia), to perform an antiwitchcraft ritual before the twenty-fourth day of the month. The *āšipu* replies, in part, as follows: "We cannot make it; the tablets are too numerous, (god only knows) when they will be written. Even the preparation of the figurines which the king saw (yesterday) took us 5 to 6 days."[11] The text again reflects how the complexity of Mesopotamian polytheism resulted in a labor-intensive system of rituals that affected the availability of the healers to the king as well as the schedule of rituals. Even with helpers, one type of consultant could not always accomplish the numerous tasks needed for exorcism in the time requested by the king.

The principal effect of monolatry is, perhaps, the automatic bifurcation of a health care system into legitimate and illegitimate options. Since only one god can be approached for healing, all other gods, whether they are believed to exist or not, are automatically rendered illegitimate. In theory, then, monolatry offers fewer options.

At the same time, a monolatrous system theoretically simplifies the search for the healing deity and thus simplifies the liturgy as well. Since only one sender/healer of disease is possible, the liturgy is reduced to appeasing or contacting only one deity. For example, in the biblical story of Elisha and Naaman (2 Kgs 5:11) the expected ritual for curing "leprosy" is as follows: "He would surely come out [of his house], and he shall stand and call upon the name of Yahweh, his god; and he shall wave his hand over the [afflicted] area; and he shall remove the 'leprosy.'"[12] No long liturgy is expected, and the only deity that has to be consulted is Yahweh. Similarly, the healings by Jesus are quite simple, requiring a short prayer to the one God. Since rituals for many gods are in principle eliminated, economic costs may be reduced.

We cannot oversimplify the effects of monolatry, however. Even in apparently monolatrous systems, such as Catholicism, patients can resort to a variety of saints and lengthy prayers (repetition of rosary prayers) that can render therapeutic rituals complex. The large number of saints can become the equivalent of the numerous gods to which one could appeal in frankly polytheistic systems. Likewise, some forms of Judaism in the first century approached polytheism in their therapeutic strategies (see below).

ETIOLOGY

Most health care systems have a theory about the causes of illness, and understanding that theory is vital for illuminating the therapeutic strategies that patients and consultants will follow. Indeed, in many health care systems, the etiology is the primary determinant in choosing a therapeutic option.

One of the most prominent typologies for etiologies was developed by George Foster, a medical anthropologist who has found it useful to identify two basic types of etiologies: naturalistic and personalistic.[13] Personalistic etiologies ascribe the cause to an active personal agent, usually a spirit or deity, while naturalistic etiologies usually ascribe the cause to a loss of equilibrium of natural substances. For Foster, personalistic etiologies have a higher degree of religious involvement than naturalistic etiologies. Responsibility for the illness resides with the patient in naturalistic etiologies, while responsibility for the illness is beyond the patient's control in personalistic etiologies.

Pilch has rightly argued that Foster's system can be refined for application to the New Testament by subdividing personalistic etiologies into illnesses in which (a) a malevolent spirit is involved and (b) no malevolent spirit is involved (although God is or might be so perceived).[14] Foster's etiologies also need refinement in other aspects. For example, Foster's idea that a personal agent is responsible for an illness does not really coincide with the degree of patient responsibility seen in the ancient Near East. Some gods may send illnesses because a patient has sinned (and so the patient is deemed responsible), or because the gods are simply capricious (and so the patient is not deemed responsible). While the division into personalistic and naturalistic etiologies may be useful, we must be more specific in the various subcategories and implications of these basic types.

PURITY AND THE SOCIORELIGIOUS
STATUS OF THE PATIENT

Within any health care system a patient bears a socioreligious status, which may be defined as the degree of negative or positive approval that a society or religion bestows upon a patient who is ill. Alternatively, one may see this status as the degree of permissible participation in the social and religious institutions of the society.

The socioreligious status of the patient, in turn, affects the options
that a health care system allows to the patient. The socioreligious status of a patient is most often expressed under the general category
known as "purity."

Since the concept of purity has engendered much discussion,
its role must be clarified here. In general, two views may be con-
trasted. One view sees purity as a primarily ideological system that
has socioeconomic consequences for the patient. A foremost advocate of the ideological basis of purity in health care is Pilch, following
the theories of Douglas, Florence Kluckhohn, and Fred Strodtbeck.[15]
The other view, advocated here, is that purity is primarily a dynamic
expression of socioeconomic judgments.[16]

Pilch links his concept of purity to the model developed by
Kluckhohn and Strodtbeck.[17] This model categorizes responses to
common human problems. One of these problems centers on how a
community should judge the value of activity. For Pilch, there are
three ways to judge the value of activity: (1) doing, which values
doing things, and personal achievements; (2) being, which judges
persons by who they are rather than what they do; and (3) being-in-
becoming, or the type of "activity that has as its goal the development
of all aspects of the self as an integrated whole."[18]

Pilch argues that purity is best associated with states of being:

> Life, moreover, in a good state of being (e.g., clean, pure, whole) is
> preferable to life in an undesirable state of being (e.g., unclean with
> leprosy, blind, deaf, mute). Hence in [Luke] 5:12–16 and 17:11–19
> Jesus restores lepers to a clean state of being. . . . Healed paralytics in
> the Bible did not go job hunting the very next day. Healing was viewed
> as restoration to integrity and wholeness, not necessarily to func-
> tion. . . . Persons who have a blemish, who are blind or lame, have a
> mutilated face or a limb too long, an injured foot or hand, a hunch-
> back, a dwarf, a sight defect, an itching disease or scabs, or crushed
> testicles are certainly capable of "doing." But their specific condition
> describes a state of unworthiness, and thus they are not permitted to
> join in the social behavior of group worship of God. Again, the issue is
> one of a state of unworthiness not the loss of bodily activities.[19]

For Pilch, it is not the ability to perform certain activities that leads to
the label "impure"; rather, the evaluation of "unwholeness" is the
basis of that label. In short, for Pilch, it is not a person's inability to
execute some socioeconomic function that brings about the label
"impure"; rather, this label brings about exclusion from important
social functions.

There are difficulties with Pilch's position. First, Pilch seems to assume that bodily wholeness and socioeconomic function are mutually exclusive categories. Contrary to Pilch's statement, the deaf, the blind, and the lame are certainly not capable of "doing" certain things that a society may value. One can just as easily argue that these persons are judged to be unwhole precisely because they are unable to perform many of the socioeconomic functions expected of a whole and healthy person in a particular society. In other words, wholeness can equal the ability to perform certain activities, the ability to "do."

In some Jewish traditions the inability to do is clearly identified as the reason for classifying certain conditions as unwhole. Thus 4QMMT 52–54, objecting to opponents who allowed the blind and deaf to partake of sacred food, notes, "And concerning the deaf who have not heard the laws and the judgments and the purity regulations, and have not heard the ordinances of Israel, since he who has not seen or heard does not know how to obey (the law); nevertheless they have access to sacred food."[20] In other words, the blind were deemed unworthy and impure by the author of *Miqsat Ma'aseh ha-Torah* because they were incapable of doing the particular activity of reading or following the law. As Qimron and Strugnell note, the blind were seen "as incapable of carrying out certain practices."[21]

In addition, Pilch generally overlooks the fundamental changes that occurred with the rise of the state and other suprafamilial organizations that had the power to define the worth of human beings. Indeed, the rise of a set of suprafamilial organizations, denominated collectively as "the state," brought a radical innovation in the relationship of the disabled individual to society.[22]

Within purely kinship-based societies there might be sufficient emotional compensation to offset any purely economic loss attributable to a physically impaired person. For example, in kinship-based societies a family may decide to maintain a disabled child because the love for the child might outweigh any economic loss of labor and income that such a child may incur. Within a kinship group, ascribed status—for example, the fact that one is a mother or father—rather than personal achievements, is the basis for evaluation of a person. In such cases, a physical disability in a person may matter less than the emotional services rendered by this person as a mother or father.

Suprafamilial organizations, on the other hand, could evaluate the socioeconomic liability of disabled individuals without any necessary consideration of emotional compensation. One example of the economic evaluation of sick individuals is found in Plato's discussion of Asclepius's evaluation of the sick: "But if a man was incapable of living in the established round and order of life, he did not think it worthwhile to treat him, since such a fellow is of no use either to himself or the state."[23] With the rise of the state, persons to whom the disabled were not directly related by kinship could decide the fate of the disabled. Henceforward, the definition of a disability was dominated by the state or by a triangular relationship between the family, the state, and the individual.

In contrast to Pilch, who dismisses the idea that a paralytic would be looking for a job the next day, restoration of health in the Greco-Roman world was important because it restored a person to function and employment. Plato comments, "A carpenter . . . when he is sick expects his physician to give him a drug. . . . But if anyone prescribes for him a long course of treatment with swathings about the head and accompaniments, he hastily says that he has no leisure to be sick, and that such a life of preoccupation with his illness and neglect of work that lies before him isn't worth living."[24] Gainful employment is a significant part of the reason that persons seek healing.

In the first century, the importance of the socioeconomic function of individuals can be seen clearly in the epitaphs of the domestic staff of Livia, the wife of Augustus. The names of these staff members are usually accompanied by their jobs in the household. More than seventy-eight distinct functions are categorized, and these include cooks (coci), carpenters (fabri), goldsmiths (aurifices), and shoemakers (calciatores).[25] People were largely defined by what they did. Contrary to Pilch, being was coterminous with function.

The importance of socioeconomic function is also reflected in the story of the centurion in Matt 8:5–10.

When he entered Capernaum, a centurion came to him, appealing to him and saying, "Lord, my servant is lying at home paralyzed, in terrible distress." And he said to him, "I will come and cure him." The centurion answered, "Lord, I am not worthy to have you come under my roof; but only speak the word, and my servant will be healed. For I also am a man under authority, with soldiers under me; and I say to one, 'Go,' and he goes, and to another, 'Come,' and he comes, and to my slave, 'Do this,' and the slave does it." When Jesus heard him, he was amazed and said to those who followed him, "Truly I tell you, in no one in Israel have I found such faith."

The author of Matthew may have wished to develop an analogy between the centurion's ability to execute orders by speaking directly with humans and Jesus' greater ability to execute commands at a distance. Still, the centurion's note that the servant was lying paralyzed shows a concern with the slave's inability to do his normal tasks.

The basis of the centurion's power is stated to be his ability to tell his servants to do something when he commanded them. One may argue that a principal purpose of this healing, at least from the centurion's viewpoint, was the restoration of a person who could again do what he was commanded to do. This study will show more fully below the importance of socioeconomic function in defining the religious status of patients in the Israelite health care systems and in the first century.

THERAPEUTIC STRATEGIES

At the most general level, a health care system may have legitimate and illegitimate recourses, especially a health care system within a larger monolatrous religious framework. Polytheistic systems may have such divisions as well, but at lower levels of the system (e.g., some herbs may be seen as good and others as harmful or ineffective). Therapeutic strategies in all health care systems form a hierarchy that usually begins with the most inexpensive and simplest options and moves toward more complex and expensive options if previous ones are unsatisfactory.

The simplest, and usually first, step in a therapeutic hierarchy of almost any health care system is self-help. In antiquity, self-help may have involved taking some readily available herb, reciting a prayer, or perhaps preparing some type of meal. The next steps may be more varied and can range from visiting a temple to calling specialized consultants. Such consultants could provide anything from diagnoses to more complicated surgical procedures. In general, patients reserve more complicated, expensive, and painful treatments as their last options.

RITUAL STRUCTURE AND COMPLEXITY

Within a therapeutic hierarchy, the complexity of a ritual influences the options that patients choose. As noted above, complex rituals, requiring numerous materials and consultants, may be expensive and even exhausting for patients. At the same time, the complexity of a ritual, with its promise to appease as many gods as possible in polytheistic systems, provides an engine for complexity.

Liturgy and healing were intimately intertwined throughout the ancient Near East. For our purposes, the term "liturgy," as it pertains to healing, refers to a ritual or a set of rituals intended to maintain or restore health.[26] Three basic types of liturgy may be distinguished in connection with illness: petitionary, therapeutic, and thanksgiving.

A liturgy may be said to have a *petitionary* function if its primary purpose is to petition for healing or the prevention of illness. The petitionary function may include the request for oracles concerning the prognosis, and not simply the petition for healing itself. If, in addition to simple petitions, a liturgy is designed to restore the ill, then the liturgy may be said to have a *therapeutic* function. The liturgy, for example, may integrate the application of medical materials, surgery, exorcism, incubation, and the performance of other rituals and procedures that are part of the therapy. A *thanksgiving* liturgy is intended to thank the deity that the patient believes is responsible for the healing. This may be something enjoined by the cult or an optional practice.

These liturgical types may also reflect broader socioreligious aspects of a health care system. Thus health care systems in which a patient is seen as too impure to enter a temple will not have temples that function as direct therapeutic centers. The temple instead may focus on petitionary and thanksgiving liturgies. This was the case with the Levitical health care system, which did not allow "lepers" in the temple. The temples of Asclepius, however, which allowed lepers in, had all three types of liturgies available. Accordingly, how Christianity viewed these liturgical types will form part of the exploration into the role of health care in the rise of Christianity.

ECONOMICS

Economics plays a large role in determining which options patients will choose.[27] One of the most important economic considerations is the fee charged by consultants. Such fees can involve anything from tangible goods to conventional currency. Individual consultants are not the only ones to impose expenses on the patient. Some of temples of Asclepius, for example, often required or suggested that patients bring animals for sacrifice.

Consultants also allocate their resources depending on economics. Some consultants may have been in the employ of only elite or royal personnel. Kings sometimes redistributed their physicians for political purposes. The consultants in some regions may be more mobile because they might not make a living by staying in a single place.

In addition to direct fees, expenses can be incurred by traveling to a healing shrine, by procuring herbs, or by the loss of wages. A modern example may be seen in a study of health care in a rural area of southern Mexico. Linda Hunt, the principal investigator, concludes, "For people who have little cash income, the cost of travel and related expenses can be prohibitive. Additionally, many rural poor people fear Mexico City as a dangerous and confusing place."[28] As in the case of the Mesopotamian ritual complexity, the number of gods and demons that needed to be appeased or repelled added to the costs in the ancient world. Modern examples of the impact of the cost of ritual paraphernalia appear among the *fallāhin* (peasants) of Egypt, who may spend a large proportion of their income on the various amulets, rituals, and spells bought from specialists.[29]

GEOGRAPHICAL ACCESSIBILITY

Where health care is dispensed helps determine which options patients choose and how health care is distributed within a society. Since, in general, patients choose the closest and most convenient resources, health care usually begins at the home in most therapeutic strategies. Patients may travel longer distances if home care is not satisfactory, and provided other factors, such as physical mobility and economic resources, are feasible.

Outside the home, we may distinguish immobile and mobile resources pertaining to geographical accessibility. On the one hand, immobile resources generally include temples, hospitals, and other resources that have a fixed location and so require a movement of the patient to that location. Mobile resources, on the other hand, move toward the patient's location. For the most part, mobile resources include itinerant healers, midwives, and even couriers who bring medicines.

TIME

When health care can be administered can affect therapeutic procedures as well as the range of the patient's options. Time limitations may be imposed in a variety of ways. Perhaps one of the most noted is the availability of consultants. Consultants may not always be available when the patient requests or needs them. We have seen how the availability of consultants was often related to the types and labor needs of certain polytheistic therapeutic rituals. Recent demographic studies show that certain times of the year brought more illnesses than other times; thus, certain times of the year probably required more physicians. Healing temples might not always be open. There might be calendrical restrictions as well. The propriety of healing on particular days of the week or month was an issue between Christianity and other forms of Judaism (see below).

SUMMARY

Although a health care system can have more components than those we have highlighted, these will be sufficient to illustrate how the health care system evinced in early Christianity differed from its counterparts. Again, although each of the individual components may be found in other health care systems, it is the combination and/or emphasis of particular components that renders each system distinctive.

CHAPTER TWO

CHAPTER TWO

The Israelite Health Care Systems

As do most nations, Israel had a variety of health care systems that experienced an evolution. The biblical materials reflect this variety, but we must remember that the canonical texts are a selective corpus that often may distort information about competing health care systems. When we speak of Israelite health care, therefore, we are really speaking of the type of health care systems advocated by the authors of the canonical texts, even though such health care systems may not have been the most prevalent or acceptable to most of the Israelite populace.[1]

THE SOCIORELIGIOUS FRAMEWORK

Israelite health care systems approved in the canonical texts were monolatrous. Accordingly, these systems were also divided into legitimate and illegitimate options. The legitimate options were those associated with Yahweh, the only legitimate god for the Hebrew canonical texts. The main source of data is the Hebrew Bible, with supplementary information provided by archaeological finds and some extrabiblical writings.

If we follow George Foster's terminology, the basic etiological system of ancient Israel was personalistic. The ultimate control of all illnesses in the Hebrew Bible rested with a personal agent, a divine being named Yahweh. Exodus 4:11, for example, contains the following observation by Yahweh: "Who gives speech to mortals? Who makes them mute or deaf, seeing or blind? Is it not I, the LORD?" Similarly, Job 5:18 states, "For he [Yahweh] wounds, but he binds up; he strikes, but his hands heal." Seemingly natural causes, such as accidents, were usually seen as instruments of Yahweh.

The Hebrew Bible has at least two principal explanations for illness. According to Deuteronomy 28, health (Heb. šālôm) encompasses a physical state associated with the fulfillment of covenantal stipulations that are fully disclosed to the members of the society, and illness stems from the violation of those stipulations.

> If you will only obey the LORD your God, by diligently observing all his commandments that I am commanding you today, the LORD your God will set you high above all the nations of the earth; all these blessings shall come upon you and overtake you, if you obey the LORD your God. (Deut 28:1–2)

Illness results from the violation of the covenant stipulations:

> But if you will not obey the LORD your God by diligently observing all his commandments and decrees, which I am commanding you today, then all these curses shall come upon you and overtake you. . . .

> The LORD will send upon you disaster, panic, and frustration in everything you attempt to do, until you are destroyed and perish quickly, on account of the evil of your deeds, because you have forsaken me. The LORD will make the pestilence cling to you until it has consumed you off the land that you are entering to possess. The LORD will afflict you with consumption, fever, inflammation, with fiery heat and drought, and with blight and mildew; they shall pursue you until you perish. (Deut 28:15–22)

The book of Job offers a contrasting, yet complementary, view, which argues that illness may be rooted in divine plans that may not be disclosed to the patient at all, and not in the transgression of published rules. The patient must trust that God's undisclosed reasons are just.

THE SOCIORELIGIOUS STATUS OF THE PATIENT

As noted above, the socioeconomic status of a patient was expressed by the terminology of *purity*. Illness conferred a generally negative status on the patient in the canonical Hebrew texts. The notion that illness produced impurity, however, had a historical evolution and some complex relationships to Israelite religious traditions.

The Levitical health care system, outlined principally in Leviticus 13–15, certainly saw those with chronic illnesses as impure. Here the focus is an illness called ṣaraʿat, which is usually mistranslated *leprosy*. The Hebrew term instead describes a wide variety of conditions with chronic discoloration of surfaces, including the walls of houses (Leviticus 13), as the main symptom. A main feature is that the condition had to be chronic to be characterized as ṣaraʿat.

The policy advocated for this chronic illness was removal from the community for as long as the disease persisted. From Lev 13:45–46 we can summarize the procedure following diagnosis:

(1) The patient shall shout out "unclean, unclean."

(2) The patient shall live alone.

(3) The patient shall live outside the camp community.

(4) This exile applies as long as the patient is afflicted.

It is clear, therefore, that purity was a consideration in the evaluation of those with chronic skin diseases. It is also plausible that fear of contagion caused "lepers" to be classified as impure. But the blind and the lame were also classified as impure, and fear of contagion alone does not seem to explain why these infirmities were considered impure. The blind and the lame were not usually perceived as having contagious diseases, yet the *Temple Scroll* forbids blind persons (כול איש עור) from entering Jerusalem "so that they may not defile the city."[2]

The best explanation lies in how the state perceived the socioeconomic value of such persons. As discussed, the state had a large role in deciding what constituted purity, on the basis of the socioeconomic value of patients. The Priestly Code certainly evaluated persons by their monetary worth (see Leviticus 26) and their productivity. As mentioned, *Miqsat Maʿaseh ha-Torah* notes that the reason for devaluation of the blind was their inability to carry out vital Jewish socioreligious practices.

The fertility of a human being greatly concerned the Priestly writers. A menstruating woman may have been assigned a sick role not only because of the loss of blood but because she was not (re)productive.[3] Infertility is not physically dangerous, but an infertile woman is unproductive insofar as the society is concerned: it means the death of the family. Clearly, this lack of productivity, not

imminent physical danger to her, is mainly responsible for her assignment to a sick and inferior role. The test for an adulterous woman in
Num 5:28 directly links being pure and being fertile: "But if the
woman has not defiled herself and is clean, then she shall be free and
shall conceive children." In short, infertile women were probably
deemed impure because they were unable to bear offspring, which
was also a family's primary means for maintaining control of land and
other socioeconomic aspects of Hebrew society.

In keeping with the intimate relationship between socioeconomic worth and the assignment of the degrees of purity, the lowest
status in the society was assigned to those who were least productive
to the socioeconomic system—the chronically ill. The idea that they
could contaminate others and the temple itself simply added to the
notion that they were a burden and a danger. This was especially the
case for patients who had severe and visible manifestations of illness.
Gradations in the ability to contribute are explicit in Lev 5:7–11. The
ill, however, were not simply the least able to contribute; they were
also a burden in other ways that made them even more vulnerable to
exclusion.

The priestly establishment, which constituted perhaps the most
important suprafamilial organization in Hebrew society in the Second
Temple period, may have sought to classify as impure the members of
society who posed the greatest socioeconomic burden and who were
the least socioeconomically productive members of society. The common denominator in the illnesses classified as impure—"leprosy,"
blindness, and musculo-skeletal disorders—is precisely their chronic
condition, with the perception that such individuals could not contribute to the social and economic welfare of the state.

Such an attitude did not differ much from the attitude, described in Plato's *Republic*, of some philosophers toward the chronically ill: "They thought that the life of a man constitutionally sick and
intemperate was of no use to himself or to others, and that the art of
medicine should not be for such nor should they be given treatment
even if they were richer than Midas."[4]

In effect, the Priestly Code advocated a health care policy by
which the state unburdened itself completely of the care for at least
some of the chronically ill. Like the attitude expressed in Plato's *Republic*, Leviticus shows little concern with medically treating such
patients. Any medical treatment may have been viewed as either
wasteful or ineffective.

If illness is seen, as in Deuteronomy and Leviticus, as a reflec-
tion of a patient's moral inadequacy or lack of purity, then illness

conferred a stigma. In Ps 38:11–12, a patient apparently complains that his condition is cause for friends to abandon him. Illness is also a time when enemies may seek to take advantage of a patient: "My friends and companions stand aloof from my affliction, and my neighbors stand far off. Those who seek my life lay their snares; those who seek to hurt me speak of ruin, and meditate treachery all day long." Such laments are not unlike those found in *Ludlul bēl nēmeqi* and other texts from Mesopotamia.[5] We also know that an illness was a most vulnerable time for a political leader. Thus, in the Hasmonean dynasty, Aristobulus II attempted to seize power during the illness of his mother, Alexandra.[6]

The book of Job paints a most dramatic picture of the stigma of illness. All of the dialogues by his friends are intent on showing that illness is a sign of Job's sin. The fact that such an assumption continued into the New Testament is shown by the disciples' question posed in the story of the blind man in John 9:2: "Rabbi, who sinned, this man or his parents, that he was born blind?" Under such circumstances the predominant attitude toward the chronically ill may have been one of alienation and exclusion from the community.

In sum, ancient Israel had a number of health care systems available as well as a variety of notions about purity. The predominant notions, however, from the viewpoint of the state, were those found in Leviticus. The Levitical health care system generally saw chronic illness as an impurity. The sick were not to partake in worship and were not considered full members of the community.

The socioreligious status assigned to patients in the most stringent Jewish health care policies had important implications for Christianity (see below). Perhaps the most significant consequence is that these laws or norms created a discrete demographic group who lacked access to the essential institutions of their society. This demographic group, the chronically ill, became a primary pool of potential new converts for Christianity. The Levitical health care system, therefore, precipitated a crisis in health care among Jewish sects, chief among them the sect eventually identified as Christianity.

THERAPEUTIC STRATEGIES

Monolatrous health care systems automatically divide the world into legitimate and illegitimate options. Since not all options are legitimate in a monolatrous system, it may be seen as more restrictive than a polytheistic one. Still, within monolatrous systems one has a number of options. As portrayed in the Hebrew Bible, self-help, usually the first option in any therapeutic hierarchy, most often was simple prayer to Yahweh. As mentioned, this is the most economical form of therapy available to a patient.

Since illness was usually deemed due to the patient's transgressions, therapeutic prayer usually entailed the review of one's actions in light of the covenant or other known rules of life. Patients spent time reminiscing about their lives and attempting to identify possible sins. An example of such a prayer is Ps 38:1–5:

> O LORD, do not rebuke me in your anger, or discipline me in your wrath. For your arrows have sunk into me, and your hand has come down on me. There is no soundness in my flesh because of your indignation; there is no health in my bones because of my sin. For my iniquities have gone over my head; they weigh like a burden too heavy for me. My wounds grow foul and fester because of my foolishness.

Confession is a crucial part of the therapy, as indicated in verse 18: "I confess my iniquity; I am sorry for my sin."

Aside from prayer, another example of self-help may be reflected in the combs found in Megiddo and other places in ancient Israel. They were apparently meant to remove ectoparasites that could be significant vectors of disease.[7] Yet another example of self-help is seen in Gen 30:14: Leah, who strives to maintain her fertility, avails herself of (דוּדָאִים, "love plants"; NRSV, "mandrakes"). The name of the plant suggests a type of aphrodisiac, although a modern botanical classification is unclear. According to the text, Leah gave Rachel these plants in return for the privilege of sleeping with Jacob. When Rachel does conceive, verse 22 says that Yahweh opened her womb (וַיִּפְתַּח אֶת־רַחְמָהּ).

The effectivity of the plant is not explicit in the text, and the author does not seem to disparage the practice of using such plants. The story shows that monolatry did not necessarily affect the legitimacy of natural remedies, and there was no reason why such plants could not be used as long as their effectivity was ultimately attributed to Yahweh. It is clear that the use of medicinal plants did not exclude attribution of their efficacy to a deity. The official religion of ancient Israel may not have objected strongly to the use of materia medica when this did not involve illegitimate consultants. Wisdom of Solomon 16:12 (ca. first century B.C.E.), however, may represent the existence of another, and perhaps equally ancient, tradition denying that materia medica (e.g., herbs) had any healing power at all.

Cross-cultural studies by medical anthropologists indicate that the use of natural remedies is a widespread mode of self-help, regardless of the socioeconomic stratum of patients.[8] In modern societies, every household usually has a range of natural remedies (insofar as these may be termed "natural")—for example, tea, chicken soup, and lemon juice—that are often selected and applied without the direct consultation of a professional.

If self-help did not provide a satisfactory solution, the next step in ancient Israel was probably to consult a healer. As early as the Amarna letters (fourteenth century B.C.E.) we have mention of the traffic of physicians in Canaanite royal courts. Since the health care system advocated by the canonical texts was monolatrous, there developed a divided system, consisting of legitimate and illegitimate options. Such healers operated independently or were based in a shrine. Temples constituted yet another consultation option (see below).

Illegitimate options, which were probably widely used by Israelites, included consultants designated as *rōpeʾîm* (2 Chr 16:12), non-Yahwistic temples (2 Kgs 1:2–4), and probably a large variety of "sorcerers" (Deut 18:10–12). Female figurines unearthed throughout monarchic Israel, especially in domestic contexts, may have played a role in fertility rituals, although it is precarious to link them with specific goddesses. The largest known dog cemetery in the ancient world, recently uncovered at Ashkelon, may be associated with a healing cult of the Persian period.[9]

The foremost legitimate consultants in the canonical texts are commonly designated prophets, and they were often in fierce competition with illegitimate consultants. Stories of healing miracles (e.g., 2 Kings 4) may reflect an effort to promote prophets as legitimate consultants. Their function was to provide prognoses (2 Kgs 8:8) and to intercede on behalf of the patient (2 Kgs 5:11). Unlike that of some of the principal healing consultants in other Near Eastern societies, the efficacy of Israelite prophets resided more in their relationship with God than in technical expertise. The demise of the prophetic office in the early Second Temple period probably led to the wide legitimation of the *rōpeʾîm* (cf. Sirach 38). Midwives (Exod 1:15–21) may actually have been the most common health care consultants, especially for pregnant women.

Both legitimate and illegitimate healing consultants may have used pharmaceuticals. Still, organic or mineral substances used for curing illnesses are rarely mentioned in the biblical texts.[10] Figs are prescribed by Isaiah the prophet to cure Hezekiah's illness (2 Kgs 20:7//Isa 38:21). Balm from Gilead is mentioned in Jer 8:22. Genesis

37:25 reports that balm was one of the commodities transported from Gilead to Egypt. Preliminary reports of the excavations at ʿEin Gedi by Yizhar Hirschfeld indicate that this town's production of balm was a major source of income.[11] This seems to confirm the biblical claims that a balm trade flourished in Palestine. We are uncertain of the extent to which surgery was used by legitimate consultants in ancient Israel. Prophets are never depicted as recommending or performing surgery. Ezekiel 30:21 speaks of the Egyptians' use of bandages for broken arms; in all probability, such procedures were not uniquely Egyptian but were known and used throughout the Near East. Archaeology, however, contributes to our knowledge. The trephined skulls found from the Neolithic period onward at Jericho and elsewhere indicate that there were surgeons in Palestine. The implantation of a bronze wire in a tooth at Horvat ʿEin Ziq, a small Nabatean fortress in the northern Negev in the Hellenistic era, attests to the existence of dental surgery.[12]

THERAPEUTIC RITUAL STRUCTURE

The therapeutic ritual structure of Israelite health care attested in the canonical texts is quite simple. Since these texts advocate monolatry, only one deity needs to be entreated in order to find the cure. The simplicity of monolatry is illustrated in 2 Kgs 5:11, which speaks of the expectation of Naaman concerning Hebrew therapy:

> But Naaman became angry and went away, saying, "I thought that for me he [Elisha] would surely come out, and stand and call on the name of the LORD his God, and would wave his hand over the spot, and cure the leprosy!"

Naaman expects no extensive rituals. Although such a ritual is perhaps not necessary, Elisha wants Naaman to submerge himself in the Jordan river seven times. The story apparently is meant to illustrate the special nature of Israel's territory, and Naaman returns to Syria with some of Israel's dust. Apparently, the author expected the reader to understand that therapeutic simplicity was the norm, and the ritual at the Jordan a unique request by a prophet.

The simplicity of Hebrew therapeutic rituals, at least in the canonical texts, is also evidenced in the story of the healing of Abimelech, the king of Gerar. Genesis 20:17 says simply, "Then Abraham prayed to God; and God healed Abimelech, and also healed his wife and female slaves so that they bore children." Again, no elaborate ritual is reported, only simple prayer.

These stories also illustrate another point about the Israelite health care system, at least as portrayed in the canonical texts. The patient's faith in Yahweh did not alone guarantee healing. Sometimes Yahweh healed only when entreated by those with whom he had a special relationship—for example, prophets such as Abraham, Moses, and Elijah.

Clearly the Israelites knew and employed more complex rituals. According to the Deuteronomistic History, the majority of Israelites were not monolatrous for most of their history. In 2 Kgs 18:5 the serpent made by Moses was being used in therapeutic rituals, apparently at the temple. According to Num 21:8–9 Moses himself had made this metallic serpent to cure snakebites. The therapeutic ritual seemed to consist simply of gazing at this metallic serpent. In Num 12:13–14 Miriam's therapy for leprosy includes her removal from the camp for seven days, even though a simple prayer by Moses was deemed to be sufficient otherwise.

The large number of fertility figurines also indicates that Israelites engaged in therapeutic practices that were indistinguishable from those of other groups in ancient Palestine. The role of Canaanite temples in fertility cults in the Late Bronze Age is well documented archaeologically.[13] The vitality of fertility cults around Jerusalem, the capital of Yahwism, in the preexilic period is attested by the large number of nude female figurines discovered in the Jerusalem area.[14] Some of those found in domestic contexts may be seen as a form of self-help. Still, as Carol Meyers notes, we cannot be absolutely certain that all figurines of women found in Palestine were used in the search for fertility.[15]

ECONOMICS

The cost of health care is often primarily exhibited in the direct fees charged for consultation services. Assessing the extent to which fees were a normal part of consultation in ancient Israel poses problems. The exchange of goods for services is seen in a number of passages in the Hebrew Bible—for example, Exod 21:18–19:

> When individuals quarrel and one strikes the other with a stone or fist so that the injured party, though not dead, is confined to bed, but recovers and walks around outside with the help of a staff, then the assailant shall be free of liability, except to pay for the loss of time, and to arrange for full recovery.

The phrase "to arrange for full recovery" (רַפֹּא יְרַפֵּא) probably included the payment of physician's fees. This well-known Hebrew construction consists of the absolute infinitive and the verb of the same root, רָפָא, which also may assume the form of a noun, translated "physicians" in 2 Chr 16:12. Unless the assailant himself was expected to render medical treatment, the phrase "to arrange for full recovery" (רַפֹּא יְרַפֵּא) probably included the payment of a physician's fees. The *Targum Onqelos,* which is supported by Rashi, is even more explicit in its translation: "He shall pay the physician's fee" (Aramaic: וַאֲגַר אָסְיָא יְשַׁלֵּם).[16]

The story of Namaan's healing in 2 Kings 5 illustrates that remuneration was generally expected for healing services. Namaan offers a present to Elisha (2 Kgs 5:15), but Elisha refuses. Gehazi, Elisha's servant, then proceeds to extract the remuneration from Namaan without Elisha's knowledge. When Elisha discovers Gehazi's plot, he indicates (5:21) that the remuneration is to be avoided only at this particular time: "Is this a time to accept money and to accept clothing, olive orchards and vineyards, sheep and oxen, and male and female slaves?" Thus olive orchards, vineyards, females slaves, and other types of remuneration seem to have been generally accepted, except in the extenuating circumstances to which Elisha alludes.

As noted above, a patient's faith in Yahweh did not always guarantee healing. Yahweh often healed only when entreated by a person with whom Yahweh had a special relationship. Accordingly, a patient might have to search for a consultant believed to have a special relationship with Yahweh. If so, a patient might have to incur expenses related to the search.

In all likelihood therapeutic rituals in Yahwistic temples were at times expensive for patients. In 1 Samuel 1, for example, Hannah and her family sacrificed part of their flock for Yahweh. When sacrifices were meant to invite Yahweh's healing, they constituted a fee for therapy. In the case of Hannah, there was a much more costly expense—her firstborn child.

With the exclusion of the ill from the temple, however, fees for therapy were automatically eliminated. Still, thanksgiving or "well-being" offerings (Lev 7:11–36) after an illness were probably always acceptable and economically advantageous for the temple. The Levitical sacrifices seem graduated according to the patient's ability to pay. Offerings after an illness also may have served as public notice of the readmission of previously ostracized patients to the society (Lev 14:1–32). The advantage of thanksgiving rituals is that they avoided the problem of any fear of contagion yet reaped the benefits of any fees paid by patients if they were healed.

GEOGRAPHICAL ACCESSIBILITY

As noted, where health care is dispensed is a crucial part of a health care system, and there are two types of resources pertaining to geographical accessibility: mobile and immobile. In ancient Israel, the principal immobile resource consisted of shrines. Because of the monolatrous religious framework, shrines were classified as legitimate or illegitimate.

It is clear that in some traditions Yahwistic shrines were allowed as therapeutic loci. For example, in 1 Samuel 1, Hannah visited the temple at Shiloh to help reverse her infertility. Second Kings indicates that, prior to Hezekiah's reforms, the temple of Jerusalem allowed the use of the bronze serpent in therapeutic rituals. The bronze serpent was made by Moses as a therapeutic device (Num 21:6–9).[17]

By the postexilic period only the temple of Jerusalem was legitimate, in the canonical view. Moreover, the Priestly Code did not allow the presence of lepers in the temple. It is likely that the blind and the lame were also excluded (see 2 Sam 5:8). As is apparent in the *Rule of the Congregation* (1QSa 2:4–9), some of the authors of the Dead Sea Scrolls explicitly excluded those with skin ailments, the blind, and the lame not only from the temple but from Jerusalem itself.[18]

The implications for accessibility are obvious. The temple could not serve as a therapeutic locus. This fact is also reflected in the story of Hezekiah, who indicates that he will visit the temple of Yahweh *after* he is healed (2 Kgs 20:5). First Kings 8 may have sought to neutralize this lack of a direct therapeutic locus by arguing that all one need do is extend the hands toward the temple in order to be healed. This was a radical idea, as it would have precluded the need for any other sort of therapeutic locus.

Despite this notion that one need only pray toward the temple, the Deuteronomistic History also advocated the employment of mobile consultants. The chief mobile resource was the prophet, at least as portrayed in the Deuteronomistic History. As noted, the prophet's function was to provide prognoses and intercede on behalf of the patient.

The disadvantages of mobile consultants such as Elijah and Elisha are obvious if their portrayal in the Deuteronomistic History bears any semblance to reality. First, since these consultants were unique, they were not available in sufficient numbers to make much of an impact on a large population, even though it would have been convenient to have one come to the patient. Second, usually the patient had to go in search of a consultant, and this search, as noted, could be expensive.

TIME

The canonical Hebrew texts indicate that health care had temporal restrictions. In Num 12:15, Miriam had to be removed for seven days from the camp before she could receive therapy. Although this particular practice may have been unusual, it is likely that many patients had to endure ritual delays before having their problems addressed directly.

Perhaps the most well-known temporal feature of Israelite health care is that it could not be dispensed liberally on the Sabbath. Although the Hebrew Bible does not directly state this, it is reasonable to assume that medical healing would constitute work, which is prohibited on the Sabbath according to Deut 5:12 and other passages. More explicit prohibitions concerning healing on the Sabbath are found in the Dead Sea Scrolls and the New Testament (see ch. 8, below).

We are able to make some inferences about the effect of other prohibitions found in the Hebrew Bible. For example, Num 15:32–36 contains the story of a man who was executed after he was found gathering sticks on the Sabbath day. Presumably, gathering medicinal plants on the Sabbath was likewise prohibited. Although this would probably not be critical when consultants already had the plants available for treatment, it might pose a problem for medicinal substances that had to be prepared as soon as they were uprooted.

Nehemiah 13:19 indicates that the gates of Jerusalem were shut on the Sabbath day. Thus, any consultants who might wish to visit a patient in Jerusalem on the Sabbath might be delayed by at least a day. Similarly, since no commerce was to be conducted in Jerusalem on the Sabbath (cf. Jer 17:27), the purchase of any needed medicinal materials would not be allowed. For the most part, however, such prohibitions against procuring or selling pharmaceuticals on the Sabbath probably did not interfere much with treatment.

If one followed the Levitical laws, there were also other temporal rules that restricted access to health care even more. Menstruation, for example, rendered women unclean for at least seven days, according to Lev 15:19. Anyone who touched her or anything on which she had lain or sat was unclean until evening and would have to wash his or her clothes and bathe. Such rules presumably rendered it exceedingly difficult for any physician to treat women during their menstrual period.

Leviticus 15:25–27 has rules that impose even more temporal restrictions on sick women:

> If a woman has a discharge of blood for many days, not at the time of her impurity, or if she has a discharge beyond the time of her impurity, all the days of the discharge she shall continue in uncleanness; as in the days of her impurity, she shall be unclean. Every bed on which she lies during all the days of her discharge shall be treated as the bed of her impurity; and everything on which she sits shall be unclean, as in the uncleanness of her impurity. Whoever touches these things shall be unclean, and shall wash his clothes, and bathe in water, and be unclean until the evening.

Blood flow does not normally indicate a disease in menstruating women. One outside of the normal menstrual period, however, is a probable indicator of disease. If we apply the rules in Lev 15:25–27, then it is likely that also physicians who came in contact with such women had to wash their clothes, bathe, and be regarded as unclean until evening. Such temporal rules would render quite difficult the medical treatment of any woman suffering from a disease of the reproductive organs.[19]

In sum, Israel had a number of health care systems during its history. The Levitical health care policies, however, seem to have become paradigmatic in the Hebrew Bible. This health care system was not geared toward the needs of individual patients; rather, the aim was to safeguard the community, at least from the perspective of the elite priesthood, which defined purity and other factors that impinged on the treatment of patients. Rules concerning women who might be suffering diseases of the reproductive organs rendered their treatment difficult. More significantly, chronically ill patients were excluded altogether from the temple and from the community itself. Thus families were separated from their chronically ill members. The use of available legitimate consultants was quite difficult as well, since they probably were not numerous. Eventually the combined negative impact of these policies for patients would become the concern of a dissenting Jewish sect that became known as Christianity.

CHAPTER THREE

Major Greco-Roman Traditions

The Mediterranean basin of the first century was teeming with a vast array of religions. Many, if not most, of them included healing in their services. In order to assess the extent of competition among these traditions, it is useful to survey briefly some of the main Greco-Roman religions, then examine in more detail the options offered by each cult in fees, geography, and the other main components of the health care systems of the first century.

ASCLEPIUS

Asclepius had a long history in Greek literature, but his origins are still obscure. The earliest mention of Asclepius is by Homer (*Iliad* 4.194), who depicts him as a highly skilled human physician. The most prevalent view of the origins of Asclepius is as a patron hero of physicians.[1] If he was originally a human being, his origins were not much earlier than Homer.

As fictive sons of the hero, physicians were called Asclepiads, although we should not assume that this epithet always implied contiguity between the temple priests and the secular physicians. It was not until the sixth century B.C.E. that Asclepius was deified.[2] At first he was simply an adjunct divinity to Apollo Maleatas, a healing god who was himself of diverse ancestry; by the fourth century B.C.E., however, Asclepius had become an independent healing god eclipsing Apollo as a healing deity, although he continued to be regarded as a son of Apollo.

It is uncertain where the earliest Asclepius temple was located. The oldest shrine, according to Strabo, was in Tricca (Thessaly).[3] Asclepius seems to have been active in Thessaly and the Peloponnese, but he was rarer in inland sites. In Boeotia another healing god, Trophonius, was prominent.[4]

The main centers of the Asclepius cult were at Epidaurus in the Peloponnese,[5] Cos,[6] Pergamum,[7] Athens,[8] and Corinth,[9] and these sites have provided much of the archaeological information on Asclepieia. Shrines are also found at Syracuse, Thasos, Delos, and Paros; all of these flourished after the fourth century B.C.E.[10] Newer material has been published from the shrine of Asclepius at Fregellae (Italy), a site that was apparently destroyed by 125 B.C.E.[11] Ephesus, a prime center of early Christian activity, had many devotees to Asclepius; archaeological evidence shows the presence of votive statues for Asclepius in public places and in private homes.[12]

The reasons for the rise of the Asclepius healing cult are not entirely clear and are undoubtedly complex. There is evidence, however, that health care crises helped the cult to expand, in some instances. The initial impulses for the proliferation of Asclepieia came during an increased incidence of disease in the fifth to fourth centuries B.C.E. The highly tentative and selective paleodemographical data studied by, among others, Angel,[13] Richardson,[14] and Grmek indicate that there was a decrease in life expectancy at the beginning of the fourth century B.C.E. Grmek reports, "The decline in average lifespan probably began in the fifth century B.C. and became apparent in the fourth century."[15] This decline may have been due to a combination of war, famine, and disease.[16] A plague that may have killed a quarter of the Athenian land army struck Athens in 429 B.C.E. A few years after this plague the cult of Asclepius was introduced there.[17] The cult of Asclepius was also introduced into Rome after a plague in 293/292 B.C.E.[18]

A rise in disease need not be the only factor, however, in explaining why certain places became central shrines for healing deities. The rise of Epidaurus may have benefited from its relative neutrality in addition to a decrease in the general health of Greece.

The fourth century B.C.E. seems to have witnessed a general socioeconomic upheaval, according to Alexander Fuks.[19] His Marxist analysis points to a social imbalance caused by the rise of a rural "proletariat" that resulted from the loss of land by numerous small farmers, who then swelled the population of cities. Fuks also argues that the change to slave labor by large wealthy landowners caused rural unemployment among small farmers.

Although critical of Marxist analyses of ancient Greek society, Andrew Lintott agrees that the fourth century witnessed a higher than normal incidence of civil strife.[20] According to Lintott, such strife, which rendered many families into homeless wanderers, was not always caused by a class struggle.[21] For him, the important factors were intercity rivalry, political maneuvering within the ruling classes (e.g., who among the aristocrats would rule), and the changing loyalties of significant pools of mercenary manpower. In any event, the famous Asclepius temple at Epidaurus came to prominence in the fourth century B.C.E. amidst rapid urbanization, civil strife, and tensions between the rich and the poor in the nearby city of Argos. With few exceptions, Asclepius was not a politically oriented deity. The specialization of Asclepius in healing was undoubtedly one factor in his evading political conflict. The Asclepius temple at Epidaurus may have been a place where patients, no matter their politics or social origins, could be seen as equals in illness. The rich and the poor, the Argive and the Athenian, were welcome in the Asclepieion.[22]

In sum, although an absolute causal link between socioeconomic circumstances and the rise of some of the temples of Asclepius cannot always be established, we can at least illuminate some of the more plausible reasons for the success of these shrines. While a catastrophic health crisis may have been primarily responsible for the rise of the temple of Asclepius at Athens, more complex socioeconomic factors may explain the rise of the shrine at Epidaurus. In any event, the rise of the Asclepius traditions highlights the importance of health care and social crises for the rise of religious movements centered on healing.

ISIS

Isis is the Greek form of an Egyptian name, usually transliterated *s.t.,* that denotes the royal throne of which she is a personification. This goddess's association with health care rendered a conflict with Christianity nearly inevitable: "A bitter struggle had to be waged before the Graeco-Roman world at last accepted Jesus instead of Isis. Among the reasons for the keenness of the conflict none was more important than the claim made by the upholders of the Egyptian faith that their goddess was a wonder-worker with the gift of healing the sick."[23]

Indeed, Isis's association with health care may be traced as far back as the Pyramid texts of the fifth and sixth dynasties in the Old Kingdom of Egypt. The conflict with Christianity is evinced as late as the fifth century. Cyril of Alexandria (376–444), for example, attempted to destroy the temple of Isis Medica at Menouthis.[24]

The Greek author Plutarch (first century C.E.) is perhaps most responsible for transmitting a coherent myth about the role of Isis in the Egyptian pantheon. In the Plutarchian version, the brother of Isis, Osiris, is tricked by Seth, his brother and archenemy, into entombing himself in a casket. The casket floats all the way to Byblos in Phoenicia. In Byblos Osiris's casket is enveloped by a tree, and eventually the local king extricates the casket and uses it as a pillar for his house. Isis searches for Osiris, and after some intrigue, Isis rescues the casket from the king. Osiris, however, is found by Seth, known also as Typhon, and dismembered into fourteen parts. Isis searches for these parts and succeeds in reconstituting Osiris, who becomes the lord of the netherworld.

As Kee notes, Plutarch uses Platonic cosmology to reinterpret the Isis-Osiris myth.[25] Osiris becomes a symbol of the relationship between the upper and lower worlds. Isis, for Plutarch, is not so much a healing deity as a symbol for the means to apprehend ultimate reality.

Plutarch's version is quite late, and it is not always feasible to identify the antiquity or authenticity of some of his material. The reconstitution of Osiris by Isis, however, is attested already in the Old Kingdom.[26] Moreover, the ability to reconstitute a body and the association with resurrection seem to be ancient motifs in healing deities. For example, Ninisina, the Mesopotamian healing goddess known also as Gula, is described as "the lady who makes the 'broken-up' whole (again)."[27] Likewise, the name of one of Gula's temples, "House of the Plant of Life" (Eunamtila), is similar to one of Isis's epithets, "Lady of the House of Life."[28] Self-congratulatory hymns for both Isis and Gula survive.[29]

The curative activities of Isis are chronicled in a variety of inscriptions. At Medinet Madi (Egypt) one inscription states, "As many as come to doom with fatal diseases having called upon you, they quickly obtain your life."[30] But as is the case with many healing deities, Isis could cause diseases as well as cure them. For example, she could blind men who incurred her wrath.[31] Thus a character in one of Juvenal's Satires exclaims, "Let Isis deal with my body as she wills, and blast my sight with her avenging rattle."[32]

The incantations for healing were sometimes incorporated within stories of healing. In one story found in the Metternich Stela (fourth century B.C.E.), scorpions sting the son of a woman who had been inhospitable to Isis. Isis, nonetheless, consents to healing the child and calls upon the poison to come forth from him. The story is interrupted in order to provide the following incantation, which might be used by a regular patient: "May the child live and the poison die. . . . As Horus will be cured for his mother Isis, those who suffer will be cured likewise."[33] The Bible also has stories including prayers that may have directed patients in their healing strategies (e.g., 1 Kgs 8:37–38).

The usual iconography of Isis depicts her with a sistrum, an instrument with apotropaic and musical functions. Plutarch remarks that the function of the sistrum is to express the idea that all things need to be shaken when they grow drowsy and torpid. He adds that it was used to repel Typhon, the enemy of Osiris.[34]

Witt observes that Isis's cult never inspired huge temples in her name alone.[35] From the Hellenistic period onward, the temples of Isis are usually associated with Sarapis, a god of still-debated origin, who apparently came to prominence during the reign of Ptolemy I Soter (305–282 B.C.E.).[36] Dedicated to both Isis and Serapis, the Serapeum of Alexandria was perhaps one of the most famous sanctuaries in the ancient world.[37]

During the first century the cult of Isis attained a significant following among many prominent Romans. The Roman emperor Vespasian (81–96 C.E.), for example, spent the night in the temple of Isis on the Campus Martius on the night before the celebration of his victory over Judea.[38] Vespasian himself is said to have healed a blind man and a cripple in the Serapeum of Alexandria.[39] Otherwise, her shrines were often associated with brothels and other services aimed at sailors.

The shrines of Isis could be found all around the Mediterranean basin. Piraeus, near Athens, may have installed Isis as early as 353 B.C.E.[40] In Palestine, figurines of Isis may be represented at a cave complex in Maresha from the Hellenistic period.[41] Antioch, an important early center of Christianity, may have initiated a vigorous cult of Isis as early as the third century B.C.E.[42] Indeed, Isis was present at many of the early important centers of Christianity, such as Ephesus, Athens, Philippi, and Corinth. The distribution of shrines in Italy may have been uneven, but the shrines at Rome and Pompeii were very well known.[43] In a sense, the geographical encounter between Isis and Christianity was inevitable in the first century.

MITHRAISM

Ernst Renan conjectured that "if Christianity had been stopped in its growth by some mortal illness, the world would have become Mithraic."[44] Indeed, it has been argued that Mithraism bore so many resemblances to Christian rituals, including baptism and the Eucharist, that the two were often confused. Many scholars think that Tertullian noted such parallels in his *Prescription against Heretics*.[45] In addition to these parallels with Christianity, Plutarch claimed that Tarsus, home of St. Paul, was also a cradle of Mithraism.[46] It is uncertain to what extent Mithraism competed with Christianity in terms of health care. Despite recent advances in the study of Mithraism, we still do not know much about the cult of Mithras, and even less about its healing practices.[47]

Mithraism spread in the first century, peaked in the third, but had experienced a significant demise by the fourth.[48] The trademark of the Mithraic tradition was the cave shrines decorated with the illustration of a tauroctony, the slaying of a bull by Mithras. Such scenes usually include other divine characters and icons that parallel elements of the zodiac. This cult was patronized prominently by military men, and women were excluded altogether. About four hundred places of Mithraic worship have been identified, ranging from Dura Europos to Britain.[49] Caesarea Maritima bears the only known Mithraeum in Roman Palestine.[50]

For most of this century, the work of Franz Cumont has dominated Mithraic studies and the interpretation of Mithraic iconography.[51] His thesis was that the Mithras known mostly from his cave shrines in Europe represented the transplantation of an older Persian deity of the same name. Cumont saw the proper interpretation of the myth of the bull slaying in, among other sources, the Bundahishn, a Zoroastrian text in which Ahriman, the principle of evil, slays a bull that bears the seeds of life within it.

The work of John Hinnells, David Ulansey, and others has reversed much, if not all, of Cumont's main contentions. There is still debate, however, about whether Mithraism is derivative of eastern religions and also about its antiquity. Ulansey, for example, champions an origin in Cilicia about the first century. Still others see roots in Iran at a much earlier time.[52] Some of the most recent work has stressed the importance of astrology and astronomy for explaining the cult of Mithras. Thus David Ulansey sees the central iconography of Mithras as a sort of star map, which guides devotees on their heavenly journeys. Nothing about the current interpretations of Mithraic iconography can be related to health care, except in the most general fashion (e.g., the well-being of the cosmos and its inhabitants).

Texts that had been used to reconstruct many of the Mithraic rituals have come under renewed scrutiny. Per Beskow, for instance, has questioned whether modern scholars have been hasty in relying on Tertullian's notion of parallels with Christianity.[53] If they have, we may know even less about Mithraic rituals than we did before Tertullian's passage was considered a valuable source.

Despite the paucity of information, we do have some indications that health care was not disregarded by the devotees of Mithras. At Vieu, a town in the Rhône River valley, for example, a physician seems to have incorporated Mithras into a bath complex associated also with Apollo, the Gallo-Roman god of healing waters.[54] But the dates and places are too far removed from the cradle of Christianity to make any inferences about competition with it. The exact nature of the health practices at Vieu are also not clear.

Despite Renan's ambitious claims, the extent to which Mithraism competed with Christianity in health care is not discernible on the basis of present information. If any Mithraic healing rituals were held in caves, it would pose problems of access and transportation. And the restriction of the cult to males alone would be a disadvantage that Christianity did not have. We have no information about Mithraism's fees, geographic accessibility, therapeutic strategies, or other issues discussed in this study.

SECULAR GRECO-ROMAN TRADITIONS

By secular traditions is meant here a variety of medical approaches that emphasized natural, not supernatural, assumptions in illness's etiology and therapy. For the most part, these approaches are exemplified in the work of a selective set of Greco-Roman figures, such as Hippocrates and Galen.[55] These traditions, in turn, were probably derived from naturalist theories of Empedocles and other pre-Hippocratic philosophers.[56] With few exceptions, however, we cannot assume that emphasis on the natural meant absolute exclusion of the supernatural. The predominant pattern was for natural and supernatural etiologies and therapies to interact in the life of the average patient.

Perhaps the most important source for our knowledge of secular medicine in the first century is preserved in De medicina, authored by Aulus Cornelius Celsus. If we follow Celsus, what may be classified as secular medicine in the first century was divided since Hellenistic times into three branches—dietetics, pharmacology, and surgery.[57]

De medicina shows that the most revered of the secular traditions of first-century Rome was still the Greek Hippocratic tradition. The adjective "Hippocratic" derives from Hippocrates, who is regarded as the father of Greek medicine. Hippocrates is usually thought to have lived in the fifth century B.C.E. Not much is really known about him, however, and what is called the Hippocratic corpus is in reality the work of a variety of authors, none of whom can be definitely identified with Hippocrates at all.[58]

A typical secularist approach to illness is illustrated in the Hippocratic treatise The Sacred Disease (Περὶ ἱερῆς νούσου); the "sacred disease" is usually regarded as epilepsy. The entire work is devoted to showing that this illness is of natural, not divine, origin. One of the arguments for a nonsupernatural origin is as follows: "Another strong proof that this disease is no more divine than any other is that it affects the naturally phlegmatic, but does not attack the bilious . . . the fact is that the cause of this affection, as of the more serious disease generally, is the brain."[59] The author was partially correct in saying that the brain was involved in this illness, if indeed it was epilepsy.[60] As will be explained in more detail below, this explanation reflects the pervasive idea that the imbalance of certain bodily substances was at the root of illness.

According to Celsus, from the time of Hippocrates on, a number of schools likewise emphasized natural explanations and divorced philosophy from medicine. The most important schools thrived in Alexandria during the Hellenistic period. Herophilus of Chalcedon (ca. 330–260 B.C.E.) and Erasistratus of Ceos (ca. 330–255 B.C.E.), both of whom are linked with Alexandria, are credited by Celsus (De medicina, Proemium, 23–34) with advancing the knowledge of anatomy through the use of human dissection.

De medicina also discusses the Empiricist school—thought to be descended from Acron of Acragas of Sicily (fifth century B.C.E.)—and its emphasis of practice over theory. Empiricists focused on identifying therapies that worked, and not so much on why therapies worked or the ultimate causes of illnesses. They rejected the use of dissection as a learning tool because dissection applied to dead rather than living subjects.

Another secularist tradition is associated with Asclepiades and the Methodical school. Asclepiades, a native of Bithynia, was active in Rome in the nineties B.C.E. None of his writings are extant, and his theories are transmitted through discussions of other authors who were often his ideological opponents. Instead of humors, Asclepiades emphasized a proper relationship between corpuscles and pores as the essence of good health.

Under the influence of the theories of Asclepiades, Themison of Laodicea (first century B.C.E.) and Thessalus of Tralles (ca. 60 C.E.) are credited with establishing the Methodical school. They claimed that after six months of training, one could understand the causes of diseases. They also rejected dissection.

Recent research has brought a new critical attitude toward the study of Greco-Roman medicine. In the past, modern scholars were too ready to accept Galen and other writers as reliable sources.[61] Nutton, for example, rightly cautions that we should not rely exceedingly on Galen and other relatively late authors for information about the alleged distinctions among Cos, Cnidus, and other supposed schools of medicine in the Hellenistic era.[62]

Even if there were a variety of schools, some medical historians would argue that there was very little difference in their therapeutic strategies. Thus Sigerist claims, "All early Greek medical schools differed in theoretical points, but their basic approach was very similar because they were contemporary and had common origins."[63] The principal health care strategy was the prescription of the proper diet and regimen. In short, preventing illness was the key to health. That proper diet was conducive to health is perhaps something on which Christians and non-Christians could agree. But the manner in which secular individuals and Christians proceeded once illness struck was quite distinct and in conflict on many issues.

The competition between the secular and the early Christian approaches to health care is perhaps best seen in the work of Galen, who was born in Pergamum in 129, during the reign of the emperor Hadrian. Galen was educated in Alexandria and practiced in Pergamum and Rome. According to Nutton, his notable advances related to his use of anatomical knowledge in his approach, even if this was derived from veterinary dissections rather than human ones.[64]

Galen explicitly attacked Christian health care approaches as part of his larger attack on Christian epistemology.[65] In one text, extant in an Arabic translation, Galen says, "If I had in mind people who taught their pupils in the same way as the followers of Moses and Christ teach theirs—for they order them to accept everything on faith—I should not have given you a definition."[66] This attack indicates that Galen perceived there was in the late second century a sufficiently coherent Christian philosophy showing continuity with the New Testament's emphasis on faith. Such coherence is another indication that Nutton's view of early Christian health care as compatible with secular Greco-Roman traditions is overstated. How Christianity fared in its conflict with secular health care approaches will be discussed more fully below.

SUMMARY

Some of the major religious traditions of the Mediterranean had healing as a central component. It was virtually inevitable, therefore, that conflict would arise between Christianity and these traditions. Likewise, the first and second centuries bore secular healing traditions, whose advocates (e.g., Galen) specifically opposed Christian philosophy. Christianity, as we shall see, sometimes adapted, and sometimes critiqued and rejected, specific aspects of these religious and secular traditions. Moreover, there is evidence that Christian health care formed a sufficiently coherent system that could be compared with religious and secular traditions of the Greco-Roman world.

CHAPTER FOUR

The Socioreligious Frameworks

THE BASIC SOCIORELIGIOUS FRAMEWORK

We have noted that a religious framework interacts with the health care that a society provides for its members. While a religious framework may contain a wide variety of permutations, it is useful to begin with the distinction between polytheism and monolatry, the simplest distinction relevant to health care.

For all intents and purposes, most of the major Greco-Roman religious traditions were polytheistic. Insofar as patient options are concerned, polytheism offers a much wider variety than monolatry. Even when a patient might predominantly worship or be devoted to Asclepius, for example, there was no penalty for entreating Isis, Apollo, or other healing deities.

As noted above, monolatry automatically divides a health care system into legitimate and illegitimate options. Patients are prohibited or discouraged from using health care associated with many gods. While such restrictions may have certain disadvantages for patients, the search for a sender of disease is also greatly simplified, as now there is only one deity to be entreated. Likewise, rituals can be simplified, as there are not many gods requiring special paraphernalia or prayers.

Not surprisingly, of all the religious traditions of the first century in the eastern Mediterranean, Judaism is usually seen as the paradigmatic monotheistic system. There is significant debate, however, about whether Judaism—if one can speak of such a homogeneous entity—was monotheistic in the first century. Indeed, many

Jews felt no compunction about accommodating to a polytheistic milieu. For example, a legal contract at Gorgippa, in the region of the northern Black Sea, addresses the Jewish "most high God" but also acknowledges, in another portion, Zeus, Ge, and Helios.[1] Many might contend that such accommodationism was not true Judaism.

Peter Hayman, however, has argued that the development of Jewish angelology, particularly in Second Temple literature, renders monotheism an inappropriate description of at least some forms of otherwise traditional Judaism during the first century, not to mention other periods.[2]

Even in the Bible divine figures are sometimes substituted for Yahweh when the latter's action might seem questionable, as in the case of Yahweh's apparent attack on Moses in Exod 4:24–26. *Jubilees* 48.2 substitutes Mastemah for Yahweh when alluding to this episode in Exodus. This is not unusual given the substitution of Satan (or a Satan) in 1 Chr 21:1 for Yahweh in 2 Sam 24:1, in an episode that apparently represents Yahweh as the cause of a census later punished as a sin.

Likewise, in the Bible there are many divine entities besides Yahweh, serving as intermediaries between Yahweh and human beings. Intermediation, after all, is a well-known biblical tradition, exemplified by such revered figures as Abraham (e.g., Genesis 18) and Moses (e.g., Numbers 12). Many angels are sent to help human beings (e.g., Judges 13). Such angelic help is also extended to health care, even if the ultimate healer is a single deity, Yahweh (see below).

The foregoing discussion indicates that, if monotheism refers to the role of only Yahweh in the healing of illnesses, then many forms of Judaism in the first century were not absolutely monotheistic. As we shall show more clearly in chapter 5, a variety of divine beings other than Yahweh played a legitimate role in the healing of illnesses in many forms of Judaism. Early Christianity, as we shall see, differed in attempting to simplify this situation by acknowledging only God or Jesus as the healing deities to be entreated.

ETIOLOGY

The cause of illness, of course, often determines the treatment the patient receives. With some notable exceptions (e.g., the Empiricists), most health care systems have an etiology, or theory about the causes of disease. Perhaps the most common etiology in the Mediterranean involves supernatural personal agents. Identifying the correct sender of disease in the Greco-Roman world could be as complicated a process as the one we have identified in Mesopotamia. Any of a number of deities could be responsible for sending an illness in Greco-Roman religious traditions. As mentioned above, sometimes the same deity could both cure and cause disease—such as Isis.

Although in Judaism Yahweh is ultimately responsible for illness, it is clear that a variety of demons and supernatural beings were active in human affairs. See, for example, Rabbi Huna's comments on Ps 91:7: "Everyone among us has a thousand demons on his left hand and ten thousand on his right."[3] It seems as if most forms of Judaism believed in demons as a cause of disease. In *Testament of Solomon* 18, which may have been originally a Jewish work composed as early as the first century, there are thirty-six demons corresponding to illnesses of specific areas of the body. Some examples are:

Demon	Area of Body
Ruax	head
Artosael	eyes
Oropel	throat
Sphandor	shoulder

Some of the Dead Sea Scrolls also indicate that a variety of demons could be responsible for disease. The incantation formula in 4Q560, for instance, is apparently intended to repel, among other entities, "The male Wasting-Demon, the female Wasting-Demon," and diseases that may have been synonymous with the names of the demon (e.g., "Fever, and Chills, and Chest Pain").[4] As here, Judaism sometimes did not differ much from frankly polytheistic religions in attributing disease to supernatural beings.[5]

The numerous stories of demon possession in the New Testament vividly attest that early Christianity also assumed that demons could cause disease. Demons are responsible for conditions ranging from what may be epilepsy to paralysis. For example, in Mark 5:9 the main locutor for the demons says, "'My name is Legion; for we are many.'" Concerning the origin of the enemies of Christianity, Paul says (Eph 6:12), "For our struggle is not against enemies of blood and flesh, but against the rulers, against the authorities, against the cosmic powers of this present darkness, against the spiritual forces of evil in the heavenly places." Christian etiology thus did not differ much from that of other Jewish traditions in the role of demons. As argued below, what may be distinctive in Christianity is the relative simplification of its therapeutic strategy despite the belief in a variety of demons as causes of disease.

Sin was viewed as another cause of illness throughout the ancient Near East. Sin, if defined as any behavior that is believed to displease a divine being, is not unique to either monolatry or polytheism. Accordingly, the concept of sin as a cause of illness can be found in both polytheistic and monotheistic systems. Isis has already been mentioned. The Asclepius traditions were more ambivalent. He was called the most man-loving of the gods (θεῶν φιλανθρωπότατε) according to Aelian.[6] While many gods could be so described, it appears that Asclepius rarely, if ever, struck human beings with illness. Thus, Asclepius specialized in healing to an extent that other gods did not. This was probably one of the great attractions of the Asclepius cult.

Sin was certainly a main cause of disease in Jewish traditions. This had its basis in biblical passages, notably Deuteronomy 28, where there is clearly a promise of health for those who keep the covenant, and a promise of illness for those who do not. Job exemplifies another view, which argues that sin is not necessarily the cause of illness. Nonetheless, the view exemplified by Deuteronomy prevailed in ancient Jewish etiology.

Christianity also sometimes assumed that sin could cause illness. Herod's death is attributed to a sin in Acts 12:23: "And immediately, because he had not given the glory to God, an angel of the Lord struck him down, and he was eaten by worms and died."[7] But other texts are more ambiguous. One text that has sparked debate is 2 Cor 12:7–9:

> Therefore, to keep me from being too elated, a thorn was given me in the flesh, a messenger of Satan to torment me, to keep me from being too elated. Three times I appealed to the Lord about this, that it would leave me, but he said to me, "My grace is sufficient for you, for power is made perfect in weakness." So, I will boast all the more gladly of my weaknesses, so that the power of Christ may dwell in me.

Although most commentators believe that the thorn represents a physical ailment, Hermann Binder has argued that it refers to a spiritual or character weakness.[8] If it is an illness, then it seems clear that the cause is not sin but, rather, God's plan to glorify himself through Paul.

Also enigmatic is Jesus' admonition to the paralytic whom he healed in Mark 2:5. "When Jesus saw their faith, he said to the paralytic, 'Son, your sins are forgiven.'" Some scholars interpret this to mean that Jesus believed that sin was the cause of the paralysis.[9] It is perfectly reasonable to assume, however, that Jesus forgave this paralytic's sins regardless of their ties to the illness. The patient simply provided an opportunity for Jesus to show his authority to forgive sins; this opportunity could have been provided by any other person, sick or healthy.

Some Christian texts explicitly reject sin as the cause of illness in some cases. One example is John 9:1–3.

> As he walked along, he saw a man blind from birth. His disciples asked him, "Rabbi, who sinned, this man or his parents, that he was born blind?" Jesus answered, "Neither this man nor his parents sinned; he was born blind so that God's works might be revealed in him."

Here the author portrays the disciples as enunciating the dominant etiology in Judaism, that sin is the cause of illness. Jesus explicitly rejects this etiology. At the same time, the author acknowledges that sickness may be rooted in divine plans over which the patient has no control.

In many respects, then, Christianity, as depicted in the New Testament, is not radically different from the etiologies used in Judaism. Demons can cause illness. Sin can be a cause of illness. God's mysterious plans can be a cause of illness. We may, indeed, agree with Ulrich Mueller when he notes that "the attitude of early Christian communities toward the relationship between sin and sickness was not a unified one."[10] Like the tradition of Asclepius, however, Christianity seems to explicitly reject that sin is the *dominant* cause of illness. Many times illness is attributed simply to demonic entities who are acting on their own volition, not to anything the patient has done to displease God. These patients are victims, not perpetrators to be punished. Accordingly, they usually need not engage in an elaborate review to see what sin might have caused a disease. As argued below, these developments greatly simplified therapy.

Natural causes are, of course, most predominant in the secular medical traditions. Perhaps the most prevalent naturalistic theory of illness centered on an imbalance of essential bodily substances, called humors. References to humors can be seen in Hippocrates, Celsus, and Galen, among the major medical writers of the Greco-Roman era. Although the identity and number of these substances could vary, the number is most commonly put at four: phlegm, blood, yellow bile, and black bile. This configuration was first attested in the Hippocratic treatise *The Nature of Man:* "The body of man has in itself blood, phlegm, yellow bile, and black bile; these make up the nature of his body, and through these he feels pain or enjoys health."[11]

The four humors were eventually associated with four other properties (cold and hot, dry and wet) and with the four fundamental elements of all matter (earth, wind, water, fire), attributed to Empedocles. In turn, these were linked to the four seasons of the year. These associations can be depicted as follows:

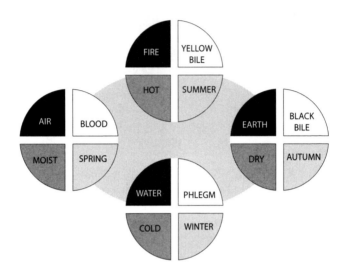

Other natural agents that could be responsible for disease might center around the interruption of airflow and other disruptions related to the *pneuma,* the substance identified with air or with breath inside the body. As already mentioned, the Hippocratic treatise *The Sacred Disease* attempted to attribute epilepsy not to the gods but to interruptions of airflow to the brain.

These natural substances and associations could be used in explaining a diagnosis and prognosis as well as in prescribing therapy. But inconsistency, and trial and error, likely predominated in practice. It is probably fair to say that, aside from these naturalistic traditions in Greco-Roman medicine, most traditions, including Christianity, saw natural factors as ultimately the instruments of a deity.

THE SOCIORELIGIOUS STATUS OF THE PATIENT

The socioreligious status of patients in the first century was a primary concern of Christianity and other Greco-Roman religious traditions. Their status was usually established according to the concept of purity. As noted, the Levitical health care system deemed as impure all those who suffered from chronic skin diseases. In addition, there is evidence that Levitical policies also deemed as impure the blind and the lame. The question becomes, To what extent were these Levitical policies continued or expanded during Christianity's rise?

Paula Fredriksen has argued against scholars who defend the idea that Jesus' main agenda was the combating of Jewish purity codes.[12] In her view, "purity does not correspond to social class."[13] We certainly must be cautious in generalizing about first-century Judaism and not assume that rules expressed in rabbinic literature about illness applied in the first century. The meager evidence available, however, indicates that Levitical precepts and rules about leprosy and other illnesses were still in vogue in the best-attested forms of Judaism in the late Second Temple period. For example, 4QMMT 64–72 states,

> And concerning (healed) lepers[14] we are [of the opinion that they may not] enter (any place) containing sacred food but should be isolated [(and) outside of any house.] And it is (indeed) written that after he (i.e. the leper) shaves and washes he should dwell outside [his tent seven] days; but now while their impurity is (still) with them le[pers enter] into a house containing sacred food. And you know [that if someone violates a prohibitive commandment unintentionally] and the fact escapes him he should bring a purification offering; [and concerning him who purposely transgresses the precepts it is writ]ten that he 'despises and blasphemes.' [Moreover, since they have the] impurity of leprosy, one should not let them (the lepers) eat of the sacred food until sunset of the eighth day. (Qimron and Strugnell)

Similarly, 11QTemple 46:16–47:11 advocates the policy that lepers and gonorrhiacs be confined east of Jerusalem.[15]

One could argue that *Miqsat Ma'aseh ha-Torah* and the *Temple Scroll* express ideals that never were executed in reality. Still, the existence, in the first century, of the policy reflected in the *Temple Scroll* may be corroborated by the notice in Mark 14:3//Matt 26:6 that Jesus met in the house of the leper in Bethany, which is east of Jerusalem. Likewise, Josephus indicates that lepers were not welcome in the Holy City in the first century.[16]

Josephus, in *Against Apion,* also shows that he considered other Levitical laws normative in the first century: "In fact, he [Moses] forbids lepers either to stay in a town or to reside in a village; they must be solitary vagrants, with their clothes rent; anyone who touches or lives under the same roof with them he considers unclean."[17] In another passage, Josephus attempts to refute Manetho's claim that the Jews were expelled from Egypt on account of their leprosy. Josephus notes that Moses would never have promulgated laws against a disease from which he himself suffered. He adds that Moses' laws were not confined to the illness of leprosy; this may mean that the blind and the lame also were included.[18]

If the laws in Leviticus were applied in at least some Jewish communities in the first century, then they created, in effect, a group of chronically ill people excluded from society. Second Kings 7 had referred to bands of lepers roving outside the city. Luke 17:11–12 indicates that such groups of lepers were also known in the first century: "On the way to Jerusalem Jesus was going through the region between Samaria and Galilee. As he entered a village, ten lepers approached him. Keeping their distance, they called out, saying, 'Jesus, Master, have mercy on us!' " Even if such a story is a literary invention of Luke, he expected his audience to accept that lepers could roam in bands.[19] This indicates that the laws excluding the chronically ill from the basic institutions of Jewish society created a new demographic group. In addition, the sick would congregate at prominent locations, such as the gates of the temple (Acts 3:2).[20] The formation of such discrete groups of chronically ill populations could serve as a ready and identifiable pool for a new religious movement.

Greco-Roman traditions also sought to rid society of the chronically ill. Suetonius states, "When certain men were exposing their sick and worn-out slaves on the island of Asclepius because of the trouble of healing them, he [Claudius] decreed that all who were exposed should be free."[21] The cost of treatment and these slaves' lack of utility clearly were the reasons they were exiled or exposed. They were deemed unworthy because of their inability to do something useful for their masters. Josephus refers to the banishment of 250,000 "afflicted persons" by Amenophis, the Egyptian king.[22] He also relates how, during the reign of Bocchoris, Egyptian temple officials, who at first welcomed the sick, decided to purge themselves of them by leading lepers into the wilderness.[23]

Josephus may be exaggerating or fictionalizing for apologetic purposes. But it is not unreasonable to argue that the chronically ill could be regarded as a society's socioeconomic burden that had to be eliminated from time to time. States unburdened themselves of these populations by declaring them impure or a danger; these populations could then be banished, killed, or persecuted in other ways. And because of the visible nature of most of the chronic illnesses discussed in this book, those who bore such illnesses constituted a discrete and identifiable demographic group.

Certain Greco-Roman religious traditions may be regarded as efforts to manage ill populations rejected by other sectors of society. Such efforts included redefining purity. The cult of Asclepius is perhaps the best example of the idea that purity is purity of the mind, not something that illness might take from the body. Porphyry notes that purity was defined as purity of thought at Epidaurus.[24] That is, thinking "holy" thoughts was sufficient to render a person pure; being physically clean or pure meant little if one's thoughts were not pure. Such a definition of purity seems to emphasize that illness itself was not an impurity that excluded one from the temple at Epidaurus. Indeed, the sick were admitted to the temple.

Similarly, in his discourse on a well associated with Asclepius, Aristides says, "This water alone is equally pleasant to the sick and to the healthy, and it is most useful for one as for the other. . . . [The water] is sacred because it saves those who use it and not because no one touches it. And the same water suffices both for purifications of what belongs to the shrine and for men to drink and be bathed in and to rejoice over when they behold it."[25] Note that purity is defined as an ability to heal. This notion of the purity of the water had the effect of inviting the sick to use the temple facilities, and it emphasized that the temple was meant for the sick. (Although purification had its place in the cult of Asclepius, it does not always seem to have been a necessary component of a healing ritual.)

At the same time, the temples of Asclepius may not have been able to manage all of the sick who sometimes were imposed upon them. This is indicated by Suetonius's report of Claudius's efforts to counteract the exposure of sick slaves on the island of Asclepius. Claudius's decree was a superficial concession that had little to do with his compassion for sick slaves. Rather, it may have been prompted by the inability of the Asclepius temples to assume the burden of sick populations. His decision favored two elite institutions (Asclepius shrines and slave masters) that may not have wished to assume the burden of large groups of sick slaves. Declaring these sick slaves free would have unburdened the Asclepius temples and the slave masters but done very little for persons who could not earn a living.

In sum, therefore, Greco-Roman traditions and forms of Judaism sought to rid themselves of chronically ill populations. The chronically ill, because of their visible physical conditions, represented a readily identifiable and discrete demographic group. Many of these, perhaps, in Jewish communities also resided in discrete and identifiable locations. This demographic group formed a ready pool of recruits and targets for the Jewish group that became known as Christianity.

Christianity represented a radical departure from attested Jewish health care approaches insofar as the socioreligious status of patients was concerned. Mark 1:40–42 offers an example: "A leper came to him begging him, and kneeling he said to him, 'If you choose, you can make me clean.' Moved with pity, Jesus stretched out his hand and touched him, and said to him, 'I do choose. Be made clean!' Immediately the leprosy left him, and he was made clean." Thus Jesus, in blatant opposition to Levitical health care policies, touches a leper. Jesus also eats in the house of Simon the leper (Mark 14:3), reflecting yet another affront to Levitical health care policies.

Indeed, Christianity attempted to redefine the concept of purity in Judaism. Like the tradition of Asclepius, Christianity did not consider patients so impure as to preclude human contact or interaction. Mark 7:15 ("there is nothing outside a person that by going in can defile, but the things that come out are what defile") reflects thoughts on purity that are much like those of Porphyry speaking of the tradition of Asclepius.[26] For the author of Mark, purity resides in the contents of the mind or heart.[27]

It seems that such activities by Jesus were meant to juxtapose Christianity with Judaism. The Gospel authors, indeed, portray the representatives of traditional Judaism (e.g., Pharisees, Sadducees, scribes) as opposing Jesus' health care practices.

It is also plain that Christianity targeted the chronically ill as a demographic group. For example, Jesus enjoins his disciples in Matt 10:8, "Cure the sick, raise the dead, cleanse the lepers, cast out demons,"[28] and in Luke 14:13–14, "But when you give a banquet, invite the poor, the crippled, the lame, and the blind. And you will be blessed, because they cannot repay you, for you will be repaid at the resurrection of the righteous." Accordingly, contrary to Fredriksen, who argues that purity did not correspond to social class, those with chronic illnesses formed an identifiable group that did not have socioeconomic privileges available to the healthy and so can be described as a class.

Luke 14:13–14 also provides a clue to the motivations for the interest in the chronically ill. Healing the sick was one of the benefits from the arrival of the kingdom of God. Thus, when John the Baptist sent envoys to ask Jesus whether he was the Messiah, Jesus' reply includes the notice that the blind and lame are being healed (Luke 7:20–22; cf. Isa 35:5–6). At the same time, the reunification of Judaism, expected near the end of the age, might have meant the removal of those obstacles that had separated the Jewish family into the sick and the healthy. Laws of purity had helped to separate people instead of unifying them.

Christianity may therefore be described as a Jewish sect that aimed to resolve a social crisis caused by the more stringent health care policies in Leviticus and other more conservative strains of Judaism in the first century. On the one hand, Levitical laws unburdened the state of responsibility for the chronically ill. On the other hand, the Levitical laws probably caused great stress in society by rupturing families and perhaps driving patients to non-Jewish health care systems. The resolution proposed by Christianity aimed not only to heal but to reinterpret purity laws so that the sick could again be part of the Jewish and human family.[29]

CHAPTER FIVE

Therapeutic Strategies

GENERAL STRATEGIES

Therapeutic strategies are an inherent element in all health care systems. As we have mentioned, such strategies are usually structured as a hierarchy. Patients first attempt to relieve their illness through self-help. Thereafter, patients might have recourse to consultants within the family, consultants outside the family, priests, and midwives and to numerous other options. On the most general level, patients have a variety of options that, in some traditions, are divided into legitimate and illegitimate categories.

For the most part, all types of recourse were legitimate in Greco-Roman traditions. There does not seem to have been a problem if a patient consulted two or more religious options, such as Isis and Asclepius. Likewise, patients in Greco-Roman traditions do not seem to have been penalized because they consulted both a secular physician and a religious healer.

In the forms of Judaism that were more monolatrous, however, the worship of Yahweh alone meant that patients were discouraged from consulting another deity. Not surprisingly, some rabbinic sources explicitly forbade healing in the name of Jesus. Thus, in one story a man named Jacob of Kefar Samma attempted to call upon Jesus ben Pantera to heal Rabbi Eleazar ben Dama, who had been bitten by a snake. But Rabbi Ishmael forbade Eleazar ben Dama from calling upon Jesus. Eleazar died before his attempt to prove that Jesus could heal him.[1]

The variety of Jewish amulets and other texts indicates that many Jews did indeed call upon deities or divine figures other than Yahweh in cases of illness. Thus the following plea is found in an incantation bowl: "May there be good healing for you from heaven in the name of El Shadday and in the name of Samakh, Asgar, Abrishakh, Samakh . . . "[2]

More elaborate therapeutic strategies are reflected in the *Testament of Solomon*. As mentioned above, this work associates specific ailments of specific areas of the body with particular demons. In turn, these demons are repelled by specific angels. Some examples are as follows:

Demon	Area of body	Angel
Ruax	head	Michael
Artosael	eyes	Ouriel
Oropel	throat	Raphael
Sphandor	shoulder	Arael

On the other hand, 11Qapocryphal Psalms[a] seems to reiterate that the efficacy of its exorcism spell rests on using the name of the Hebrew God: "In the name of [YHWH" (1:2); "Concerning the spe]ll in the name of YHWH" (4:4).[3] But even if Yahweh was ultimately held responsible for therapy, a similar appeal to figures other than Yahweh is apparent in Dead Sea Scrolls that may have been used in therapy. Thus 11QapPs[a] 4:3 states that "[Ra]phael heals them."[4] In the book of Tobit (3:17), the angel Raphael is sent to cure an unfortunate couple.

Such developed angelology means that some forms of Judaism approximated polytheistic health care frameworks. The fact that such strategies were disturbing to other forms of Judaism is evident in the following warning: "If trouble comes upon a person, let him not cry to either Michael or to Gabriel but let him cry unto Me, and I shall answer him forthwith. This is the meaning of the verse: 'whoever shall call on the name of the Lord shall be delivered.' "[5] In theory, this reduction in senders of disease could simplify rituals. Only one sender of illness needed to be sought or entreated. On the other hand, any dissatisfaction with the one deity naturally made the search for other healers attractive to many patients.

But the perceived benefits of having a variety of options in polytheism was countered by the complexity that polytheistic rituals could engender. The patient might need to engage in a lengthy and cumbersome search for many gods to find satisfactory relief. This could result in a long litany or in complicated rituals. Thus a Greek Magical Papyrus from the first century mentions Osiris, Anubis, the Dioscuri, gods of Hades, and the Eternal Mistress.[6] Paraphernalia associated with at least some of these deities seem to have been involved in the preparation of the ritual. Likewise, the developed angelology of first-century Judaism could render therapy as complex as that in polytheism. As in the case of the Mesopotamian ritual discussed in chapter 1, above, polytheism can result in complicated therapeutic ritual structures.

THERAPEUTIC HIERARCHIES

Patients throughout the Greco-Roman world used self-help of some form as a first step. Some argue that the most prominent medical treatises are, in fact, manuals of self-help for the layperson rather than manuals for professional physicians. Cato the Elder, among others, envisioned self-help as the paradigmatic form of health care. For Cato, the *paterfamilias* was responsible for the health care system of the estate.[7] The patriarch could recommend his own pharmaceuticals and offer prayers.

Simple self-help could include the use of normal foodstuffs, such as milk or eggs, for medicinal purposes. Celsus, for a case of eye trouble, states, "If neither doctor nor medicine is at hand, either of the above [eggs or milk] dropped into the eye with a little screw of lint prepared for the purpose, often relieves the trouble."[8] We may assume that all households contained at least some of the items recommended in a few of the most sophisticated medical manuals.

Consultation with a physician was probably the next step if self-help did not satisfy. The consultant might be the *paterfamilias,* as in the system envisioned by Cato the Elder. Within wealthy estates, a slave might have functioned as a physician. A list of slave specialties in the household of Livia, the wife of Augustus, bears a *medicus* (physician).[9] Other households might even be more specialized and keep a *chirurgus* (surgeon) and *ocularius* (eye specialist).[10]

Most patients in cities, however, relied on consultants based outside the home. Such physicians might be engaged in other occupations as well. Often physicians seem to have gone to the home of the sick. Both the Hippocratic tractate *Decorum* and Galen's treatise *On Physicians* assume that house calls are the common practice of physicians.

There were also some medical "taverns," *tabernae,* often indistinguishable from other commercial shops, which could cater to patients on the streets of larger towns. Some of the best known are in Pompeii (Italy). One, dubbed the "House of the Surgeon" by modern scholars, was on the Via Consolare; and another, apparently the base for a physician named A. Pumponius Magonianus, was on the famous Via dell' Abbondanza.[11]

The Hebrew Bible exhibits antipathy towards non-Yahwistic healers, as in the rebuke of Asa for his consultation of "healers" in 2 Chr 16:12. Likewise, the Mishnaic tractate *ʿAboda Zara* (2.2) warns that "one may permit heathen to heal one's property but not one's body."[12] Still, many Jews in the first century probably had no problem with consulting secular physicians. Sirach's (Sirach 38) famous praise of the physician was probably shared by many Jews in the first century.[13] Josephus does not seem to think it against his Jewish tradition to be treated by physicians in Capernaum.[14] Indeed, there was a small but significant presence of Jewish physicians in the Roman Empire.[15] Celsus himself mentions some medications ascribed to *Judaeos,* a term that may refer to a particular Jewish physician, though now unknown to us.[16]

There are also archaeological indications that professional physicians and equipment were present in Palestine. Thus a *cucurbitula,* a Roman-era medical vessel, was found at Masada, and a similar medical vessel for cupping was found at Samaria at a level dated to the Hellenistic period.[17] The presence of dental specialists is indicated by the implantation of a bronze wire in a tooth at Horvat ʿEin Ziq, a small Nabatean fortress in the northern Negev in the Hellenistic era.[18]

On the most general level, physicians were probably viewed as a valuable option for those who could afford the best care. Indeed, some authors, Seneca for instance, eulogized the value of physicians, saying that the life and good health gained from them exceeded the value of any fee.[19] We also find evidence, however, that the wide variety of consultants could also pose a problem. Patients, for example, did not know what the best advice might be. Pliny the Elder says, "Hence those wretched, quarrelsome consultations at the bedside of the patient, no consultant agreeing with another lest he should appear to acknowledge a superior. Hence too that gloomy inscription on monuments: 'It was the crowd of physicians that killed me.' "[20]

A similar complaint is voiced by Galen when he laments the disdain for the study of medicine among the upper classes: "In addition to their aversion to studying medicine, they do not consider it their duty to distinguish between the best and worst physicians."[21]

Galen adds that such a problem was even more acute in Rome "because the city is great and populous."[22] Presumably this would apply to other cities with large populations as well.

Indeed, finding a good physician was a risky procedure. Galen's treatise *On Physicians* was intended precisely to help patients identify good physicians. But he is correct in indicating that, in general, a physician of the Roman world could be almost anyone. There were no centralized certification agencies. Often physicians were transient. Reputation, more than anything, was the key to identifying a good physician, when and if that reputation could be known.

PHARMACEUTICALS

Pharmaceuticals formed an essential part of any consultant's repertory. It was for their knowledge of pharmaceuticals that most consultants were sought. That the Greco-Roman world of the first century was filled with an astounding variety of pharmaceuticals can be evidenced by the various pharmaceutical manuals produced at that time. Pedanius Dioscorides, the famed Greek pharmacologist who was active in Nero's army, collected hundreds of prescriptions in his manual, *De materia medica*.[23] Celsus's treatise *De medicina* is basically a lengthy catalog of prescriptions. Rufus of Ephesus also details hundreds of prescriptions in his manual.[24]

Some streams of Judaism in the first century had an aversion to pharmaceuticals. Thus, in a section meant to highlight the contrasts between Egyptian and Jewish healing techniques, Wis 16:12 states, "For it was neither herb nor emollient that cured them, but your word, O Lord, that heals all."[25] Most Jewish groups of the Second Temple Period, however, probably subscribed to the use of pharmaceuticals. Sirach 38:4 argues that medicinal herbs received their power directly from God. According to Josephus, the Essenes investigated the properties of medicinal roots.[26] Medicinal frankincense has been found at Masada, perhaps for use by the military troops.[27]

While the variety of pharmaceuticals may have provided patients with many options, this also could prove to be a source of confusion and frustration. The variety only reflected the idiosyncratic nature of and inefficacy of most medications. Celsus states, "But as regards to all these medicaments whether used as simples or in mixtures, their uses by medical men vary, so that it is clear that each man follows his own ideas rather than what he has found to be true by actual fact."[28] As noted below, the cost of pharmaceuticals could also be a disadvantage for many.

There were other annoyances associated with pharmaceuticals. In Apuleius's *Metamorphoses*, we find the following complaint:

> I have to put up with a husband who is even doubled over and bent with arthritis, and therefore hardly ever pays homage to Venus. I am forever rubbing his twisted and petrified fingers and burning these delicate hands of mine with smelly fomentations and dirty bandages and stinking poultices. Instead of playing the dutiful part of a wife, I have to endure the laborious role of a doctor.[29]

Thus, the preparation of medicinal substances and other inconveniences often made pharmaceuticals a disadvantage that patients might wish to do without.

SURGERY

Surgery, defined here as any procedure in which mechanical invasive methods are applied to the body, has a long history in the ancient world. We can trace the earliest surgical procedures to the trephination practices of the Neolithic Age.[30] Trephination entailed boring a hole through the skull and the consequent exposure of the brain. The procedure was also performed in the Greco-Roman era, and it is described in some detail by Celsus.[31]

Trephination was obviously an excruciating experience, and in general, all sorts of surgery in the ancient world could be quite excruciating, principally because of the lack of an effective anesthesia. Celsus describes how some painful methods of cauterizing blood vessels required burning the crown of the scalp down to the bone.[32] A common, and not much more comfortable, procedure may have been simple bloodletting: "To let blood by incising is no novelty; what is novel is that there should be scarcely any malady in which blood may not be let."[33] It is no surprise, therefore, that surgery was an option of last resort, as it is today.

In the absence of effective antibiotics and analgesics, non-surgical treatment was often something to be endured as well. One example is the cure for what is termed *dropsy* among the Greeks (*hydrōpia*). According to Celsus:

It is relieved more easily in slaves than in freemen, for since it demands hunger, thirst, and a thousand other troublesome treatments
and prolonged endurance, it is easier to help those who are easily constrained than those who have an unserviceable freedom.[34]

This comment shows that medical treatment in the ancient world
could be quite tedious, time consuming, and frustrating.

CHRISTIAN THERAPEUTIC STRATEGIES

This survey shows that Greco-Roman traditions of the first century provided a variety of options for patients. The wide array of options, however, could make the therapeutic process highly complex,
frustrating, and otherwise difficult for patients to endure. Indeed,
many of the remedies could be quite painful. As noted, polytheistic
systems tended toward complex rituals simply because of the number
of deities that might need contacting, repulsion, or appeasement.
Even in some forms of Judaism, the reliance on a variety of divine figures, pharmaceuticals, and consultants could render the therapeutic
process as complex as in Greco-Roman traditions.

Early Christianity, as evinced in the New Testament, advocated
a highly simplified therapeutic strategy that might have been advantageous to many patients, whether Jewish or not. It is true that Christianity's etiology assumed the role of a large variety of demons in the
cause of disease. It is also true that Christianity might not have
brought any more relief than any one Greco-Roman option.

Christianity, however, simplified the therapeutic process by at
least two principal concepts. Perhaps the most significant shift was a
return to a stronger form of monolatry than evinced in some of the
Jewish groups that called upon more than one divine figure. With a
sort of reformational attitude, the Jewish group that became known
as Christianity seems to have reestablished monolatry by calling on
one name again.

Repeatedly we find in Christian sources the claim that only the
name of Jesus was required to effect healing. Even Mark 9:38, which
most scholars see as the earliest Gospel, contains the notion of the
sufficiency of Jesus' name: "John said to him, 'Teacher, we saw some-
one casting out demons in your name, and we tried to stop him, because he was not following us.'" The value and sufficiency of Jesus'
name continues in Luke 10:17: "The seventy returned with joy, saying, 'Lord, in your name even the demons submit to us!'"

The emphasis on appealing to a single name in Christianity may, indeed, be a critique of, and response to, the multiplicity of names being used in the therapeutic techniques reflected in Jewish incantations, amulets, and the *Testament of Solomon*. The author of Luke–Acts may have constructed this critique by focusing the whole issue of Jesus' name in the healing of the paralytic (Acts 3–4). The episode begins at the gate of the temple, the center of traditional Judaism, where a paralytic is begging for alms. Instead of alms, the disciples bid him to stand up and walk "in the name of Jesus Christ of Nazareth" (Acts 3:6).

The use of the single name of Jesus is raised again in the speech of Peter and John before Annas, Caiaphas, and other traditional Jewish authorities in Acts 4:10–12:

> Let it be known to all of you, and to all the people of Israel, that this man is standing before you in good health *by the name* of Jesus Christ of Nazareth, whom you crucified, whom God raised from the dead. This Jesus is the stone that was rejected by you, the builders; it has become the cornerstone. There is salvation in no one else, for there is *no other name* under heaven given among mortals by which we must be saved. [Emphasis mine]

Indeed, the episode mentions the use of "the name" of Jesus ten times, an explicit sign that the author wishes to emphasize the point.

In the story of the healing of the girl with a divining spirit in Acts 16:18, we again encounter, here in a Gentile setting, the claim for the sufficiency of one name: "She kept doing this for many days. But Paul, very much annoyed, turned and said to the spirit, 'I order you in the name of Jesus Christ to come out of her.' And it came out that very hour." The sufficiency of the name of Jesus, exemplified by many healing stories and speeches, may have helped to announce Christianity's simplification of healing strategies, even if other theological purposes might have been at work.

The value of the single name of Jesus in healing continued to be a polemical issue with other religious traditions in the second century. Thus, in his epistle to the Ephesians, Ignatius denounces those who misuse, apparently for healing, the divine name: such persons are wild beasts "scarcely to be cured" (δυσθεραπεύτους), and "there is one physician who is both flesh and spirit . . . Jesus Christ our Lord."[35]

Christianity also simplified the therapeutic strategy by emphasizing the value of faith in healing. Having faith in a treatment was not a Christian invention. As noted, Wis 16:12 points to the efficacy of the "word" rather than pharmaceuticals in the cure for the serpent bites in Num 21:5–9. Likewise, the Asclepius traditions included allusions to the value of belief, although in the context of a wide variety of sometimes complex rituals.

Christianity, in comparison to Greco-Roman traditions and Judaism, was perhaps more emphatic and coherent in the notion that faith alone could restore health. That is, it was not faith in the medical treatment prescribed by a god but faith alone that could effect a cure. Despite the nuances in the use of "faith" in the Gospels, there was a relatively coherent view that faith itself was sufficient to effect a cure.[36]

The implications of a theology based on the sufficiency of faith could be quite significant in simplifying a therapeutic strategy.[37] First, such a notion could logically lead to eliminating the perceived need for pharmaceuticals. Tatian, the noted Christian polemicist of the second century, confirms the power of this logic in his portrayal of the whole pharmaceutical enterprise as a Satanic artifice: "Pharmacy in all its forms is due to the same artificial devising. If anyone is healed by matter because he trusts in it, all the more will he be healed if in himself he relies on the power of God. Just as poisons are material concoctions, so remedies too belong to the same substance."[38] Thus, for Tatian, faith in the power of God should indeed eliminate the need for pharmaceuticals. The other argument in Tatian is that remedies are as dangerous as poisons because they presumably share the same material constitution.

Nutton, among others, has argued that Tatian is an extreme case and not representative of early Christian attitudes toward pharmaceuticals.[39] Still, an aversion to the use of pharmaceuticals can already be seen in the redaction of Mark by Matthew and Luke. Crossan notes, "As with the healing medium of spittle in Mark 8:22–26, the healing medium of oil in Mark 6:13 is omitted by both Matthew 10:1 and Luke 9:1, 6."[40] A similar antipharmaceutical sentiment appears in Justin Martyr, who praises Christians able to heal patients who could not be cured by "those who used incantations and drugs."[41]

The fact remains that most of the New Testament authors rarely, if ever, substitute pharmaceuticals for, or use them in conjunction with, faith. Indeed, with the possible exception of the use of spittle, nowhere in the New Testament is Jesus seen prescribing any sort of medication. It is true that Paul prescribes wine as a medication in 1 Tim 5:23: "No longer drink only water, but take a little wine for the sake of your stomach and your frequent ailments." Yet even here it is a single medication that is prescribed for a wide assortment of ailments. Likewise, in the third century Tertullian mentions oil as the only substance used when Proculus, a Christian healer, treated the emperor Severus.[42]

Likewise, adjunct practices, such as the laying on of hands and fasting, were quite simple. The laying on of hands is a practice found already in the *Genesis Apocryphon* (1QapGen 12:29), in an episode where Abram prays for the Egyptian king (cf. Gen 20:17). In Mark 16:18, Jesus says that the laying on of hands will be one of the practices that will be performed by his followers. Although the authenticity of the passage has long been disputed,[43] the point is that the laying on of hands was never deemed to be a requirement for healing.

Fasting seems to be a requirement in some passages. In Mark 9:29, Jesus proclaims that some demons cannot be expelled without "prayer and fasting." As Bruce Metzger notes, however, the word "fasting" here (νηστεία) may be a later gloss that was resisted by "important representatives of the Alexandrian, the Western, and the Caesarean types of text."[44]

At the same time, Mark 2:19–20 (par. Matt 9:15; Luke 5:34–35) portrays Jesus as not encouraging fasting at all. These verses are part of an episode in which Jesus' disciples ask him why they don't fast as often as the disciples of John. Jesus replies, "The wedding guests cannot fast while the bridegroom is with them, can they? As long as they have the bridegroom with them, they cannot fast. The days will come when the bridegroom is taken away from them, and then they will fast on that day." Although the early church seems to have generally approved of the ritual of fasting, it does not seem part of a general therapeutic requirement.[45]

But even if the laying on of hands and fasting were required healing rituals, they were still quite simple compared with those found in Greco-Roman and other Jewish traditions. The simplicity of Christian therapeutic ritual was sufficiently widespread to enable Origen to use it as an argument against Celsus: "But even if it be impossible to show by what power Jesus wrought these miracles, it is clear that Christians employ no spells or incantations, but the simple name of Jesus, and certain other words in which they repose faith, according to the Holy Scriptures."[46] This indeed is a remarkable passage, in that Origen might be willing to concede that while the mechanisms of Christian therapeutic rituals are unclear, the simplicity of the rituals were a selling point. This simplification is not something based on some post–New Testament development but reaches back to the New Testament era. The sufficiency of faith alone and the use of one name were able to obviate the need for many pharmaceuticals, lengthy incantations, and other therapeutic strategies that could become expensive and ritually cumbersome.

EXCURSUS: MEDICINE, MIRACLE, AND MAGIC

Kee has argued that Christianity's distinction in healing was its emphasis on miracle over magic and medicine. The term "magic" has long been a subject of debate, and it is not the intention here to rehearse the long history of this debate or to enunciate a detailed case for a new definition of magic.[47] But Kee's distinction between miracle and magic is misguided and unsuccessful in explaining the distinctiveness of Christian health care.[48] The distinctive aspects of Christianity, compared with non-Christian traditions, rest on a combination of features in its health care system, but the magical vs. miracle distinction plays a minimal role.

Kee's definitions of medicine, miracle, and magic help to understand why his typology is not the key to Christianity's distinctiveness in health care:

Medicine is a method of diagnosis of human ailments and prescription for them based on a combination of theory about and observation of the body, its functions and malfunctions.

Miracle embodies the claim that healing can be accomplished through appeal to, and subsequent action by the gods, either directly or through a chosen intermediary agent.

Magic is a technique, through word or act, by which a desired end is achieved, whether that ends lies in the solution to the seeker's problem or in damage to the enemy that has caused the problem.[49]

The most significant problem here is with Kee's distinction between miracle and magic and with his correlating argument that Christianity favors miracle, not magic, as the mode of therapy.

First, some of Kee's defining features of magic can be found in Christianity. For example, there is no reason why Christian prayer cannot be seen as a "technique, through word or act, by which a desired end is achieved." Praying is a technique insofar as it includes a set of acts that are supposed to be undertaken in a proper manner so that they will work (cf. Matt 6:5–15//Luke 11:2–4). Prayer entails uttering words. Prayer centers on the utterance of words to achieve ends.

If we apply Kee's definition, prayers for healing may also involve "damage to the enemy that has caused the problem." Thus the prayers uttered by Jesus in the case of demon possession can be seen as intending to damage the demons. In Mark 5:7 the demons ask Jesus not to torment them, indicating a fear of damage. In the Beelzebul episode (Mark 3:20–30), Jesus is accused of casting out demons by using the power of Beelzebul, the prince of demons. Jesus' counterargument is that Beelzebul would not be a party to an act that damages his dominion by dividing it. In short, the casting out of Satan is implied to be an act damaging to his power.

Nor will it do much good to argue that magic centers on coercing a supernatural being to do one's will. Prayer can also be seen as an attempt to persuade and coerce the deity to do one's will. The idea that the Christian God can be coerced or persuaded through the utterance of words (e.g., prayer) is encapsulated in Luke 11:9–15:

> "So I say to you, Ask, and it will be given you; search, and you will find; knock, and the door will be opened for you. For everyone who asks receives, and everyone who searches finds, and for everyone who knocks, the door will be opened. Is there anyone among you who, if your child asks for a fish, will give a snake instead of a fish? Or if the child asks for an egg, will give a scorpion? If you then, who are evil, know how to give good gifts to your children, how much more will the heavenly Father give the Holy Spirit to those who ask him!" Now he was casting out a demon that was mute; when the demon had gone out, the one who had been mute spoke, and the crowds were amazed. But some of them said, "He casts out demons by Beelzebul, the ruler of the demons."

The discourse about the power of prayer is linked to an exorcism. In the discourse, Jesus asserts that the reason a believer may expect his prayer to be answered is that God can be seen as analogous to a parent, who acts out of love for his children. That is, requests by his children are expected to be fulfilled because the parent is constrained and susceptible to fulfilling requests out of sheer love. In sum, prayer can be seen as coercing the Christian deity to act on behalf of believers just as love coerces parents into fulfilling children's wishes.

Kee also claims that miracles are acts that focus on "the divine will at work in human experience, concerned for human destiny and cosmic purpose."[50] Such a definition assumes that the absence of explicit references to cosmic purposes in non-Christian healing incantations means that none were assumed by the "magician." For example, Kee assumes that just because the magical papyri were not explicit about larger cosmic purposes, then none must have been in the minds of the magicians. Yet incantations and other ritual procedures can often be separated from commentaries on larger cosmic purposes. Even as early as the time of Gula, the goddess of healing in the Near East, for example, we have the following statement: "May the sages apply the bandages! You (Gula) have brought about health and healing."[51] If we look solely at many healing incantations associated with Gula, we can erroneously conclude that the power of the healer resided solely in his manipulation of impersonal forces and technical skill in recitation. Yet this text recognizes that all medical procedures are in fact directed by the will of the deity. This also may be the case with the magical papyri, which often lack the mention of divine purpose found in the Gospels.

Crossan correctly says that "religion is official and approved magic; magic is unofficial and unapproved religion."[52] Susan Garrett similarly argues that the definition of magic is really culture-bound.[53] From the early Christian viewpoint, magic referred to practices and supposed miracles that relied on non-Christian deities, real or illusory. From the non-Christian viewpoint, the healing acts of Christians were performed by trickery or by some demon, as in the Beelzebul episode.

It is useful to distinguish how ancient people defined magic from how we, as bearers of a scientific method, see religion and magic. Perhaps one may also see religion and magic as analogous to theory and practice. Religion refers to an entire set of ideas that center on the human relationship with transcendent forces and beings. Magic refers to all acts by which these religious ideas are effected in the world. Thus, all therapeutic rituals are part of the magical aspect of a religion.

Accordingly, early Christianity's distinction did not reside in its emphasis on miracle over magic. And whether or not one accepts this study's definitions of religion and magic, we may still argue that Christianity's distinction was the simplification of its therapeutic ritual procedures. Simple prayer and one or two adjuncts (e.g., oil, the laying on of hands) are the most complex rituals that we see in New Testament healings. The use of aprons and handkerchiefs were clearly seen as extraordinary, and not normative in Acts 19:12. All of these simplified practices lowered the financial costs and ameliorated other practical problems found with other health care systems that had more complex ritual procedures. Moreover, the lack of fees in Christianity neutralized any charges that the healers were working for pure personal gain, as was often suspected of many healers.

CHAPTER SIX

Economics

GRECO-ROMAN TRADITIONS

The cost of health care was an important factor in ancient societies, as it is in modern ones. Cost may determine when a patient will seek help. The cost of health care may determine how many options are available to a patient. Costs may be direct or indirect and may range from direct fees to the cost of travel.

As stated, perhaps the most obvious cost was the fee charged by a physician. Not all healers charged direct fees. Some physicians were slaves attached to estates of the wealthy. Often masters "rented" out the services of these physician-slaves to others. There were also a few physicians who made a living as employees of cities. Such physicians gained a salary as well as other benefits. As Jackson notes, Julius Caesar granted citizenship to foreign physicians working in Rome in 46 B.C.E., and tax immunity was conferred on doctors in Ephesus at about the same time.[1] Some cities had public physicians who were paid by the city. But as Cohn-Haft notes, public physicians were not generally meant to offer free medical care.[2]

Healing temples could likewise demand fees for their services. Healing temples often needed significant financing to offer their services. Epigraphic evidence from Guadiz, Delos, and Pergamum indicates that the wardrobes used at the shrines of Isis could be as costly as those found in the imperial palace.[3] The numerous attendants and laborers in the larger temples only added to the financial burden that had to be transferred to clients.

The fact that healing fees within religious and secular Greco-Roman traditions could be a source of conflict and competition between health care options is evident in various periods in the eastern Mediterranean. Pliny the Elder attests to the problem that could be posed by fees within principally secular traditions. Indeed, he reports that no other art was more profitable than medicine.[4] Speaking of the consequences of establishment of the traditions of Asclepius and Hippocrates, Pliny laments, "Afterwards there was no limit to the profit from medical practice, for one of the pupils of Hippocrates, Prodicus, born in Selymbria, founded *iatraliptice* ('ointment cure') and so discovered revenue for the anointers and even drudges of the doctors."[5]

Likewise, Galen complains that quackery was rampant: "We come across rich men who have been cheated by the tricks of charlatans and those who claim to be diviners. . . . Wicked men who take up medicine are aware of this, and by coaxing the rich seek—among other things—to deceive them and to extort money."[6] Galen may not have been exaggerating much. One indication of his accuracy is that the medical training of slaves for the purpose of profiting their masters became such a crisis that Domitian (or Trajan) restricted such practices.[7] Although it is not certain that fees were the reason for his position, Aristides, the celebrated second-century devotee of Asclepius, encourages his readers not to consult physicians. He prefers going to the Asclepius temple.[8]

Aelian (ca. 200 C.E.) emphasizes that Asclepius healed the poor (τινὰ τῶν ἀπόρων ἰάσαιτο) and that the god did not receive gifts in exchange for healing.[9] Spiritual purity, not wealth, was demanded of those who came in search of healing. But many of the excavated Asclepieia indicate that they did, in fact, contain gifts of varying economic value.[10] And some of the sources concerning Asclepieia indicate that expensive gifts were also accepted, if not demanded.

Such financial demands of Asclepius temples could also be a source of conflict. Libanius (314–393 C.E.), for example, defends the necessity of paying fees to the temple of Asclepius, even if that god did not have need for wealth.[11] Libanius argues that the gods are prone to beneficence of their own free will but that they are even better disposed when petitioned and when a fee is paid at the temple. The payment of fees at the temple was defended as a means to show Asclepius the patient's goodwill rather than as a response to some need of Asclepius for wealth. Such defenses for fees show that there was a resistance to the financial demands by Asclepian hierocracies.

Through the voice of Lucius, Apuleius, the celebrated chronicler of Isis, also cites the high costs of initiation into the Isis cult: "I procured the equipment for my initiation without stint, meeting the expenses more in accordance with religious zeal than with the measure of my assets."[12] Not everyone needing a cure had to be initiated into the cult of Isis in such an intensive manner. Still, such expenses might deter poor persons, regardless of their faith in Isis, from seeking health care in her shrines.

In addition to direct fees charged by temples and physicians, many other costs added to a patient's financial burden in securing health care. In his search for a cure from Isis, Apuleius cites the costs of traveling and staying in the city as a problem for his inheritance: "The cost of my traveling had used up my modest inheritance, and living expenses in the city were much greater than my former expenses in the provinces."[13] Corinth, one of the early bastions of Christianity, had shrines of Isis and Asclepius that probably provided medical services for travelers.[14]

Pharmaceuticals also could be expensive. Plutarch mentions that physicians often recommended a medicament called *cyphi*, which consisted of sixteen ingredients, some of which were exotic and costly (e.g., myrrh, juniper).[15]

Philostratus, in his *Life of Apollonius of Tyana,* ridicules those who are ensnared by the promise of cures from exotic pharmaceuticals: "They are given all the spices which the gardens of India yield; and the cheats exact vast sums of money from them for all this, and yet do nothing to help them at all."[16] Likewise, amulets and other magical devices could be expensive, as many of them were made of gold and silver.[17]

In sum, this survey of both secular and religious health care systems shows that economics was an important concern. Fees demanded by physicians may have perhaps been the principal problem, but other costs also added to the misery and expense of health care in the first-century Mediterranean world.

CHRISTIANITY'S APPROACH TO FEES

Early Christian writers were aware of the problem that fees could cause for patients, and were openly critical of fees. This is most evident in the story of the woman with hemorrhages in Mark 5:25–26: "Now there was a woman who had been suffering from hemorrhages for twelve years. She had endured much under many physicians, and had spent all that she had; and she was no better, but rather grew worse." Luke's version (8:43–44) of the story, though less textually certain, is even more explicit about the claim that it was the physicians' fees that had left the patient impoverished: "Now there was a woman who had been suffering from hemorrhages for twelve years; and though she had spent all she had on physicians, no one could cure her. She came up behind him and touched the fringe of his clothes, and immediately her hemorrhage stopped."[18] Both versions echo at least two complaints that we have seen in Greco-Roman literature. First, physicians were not efficacious. Second, regardless of whether physicians were efficacious, they charged fees. The story mentions the devastating impact of physicians: they had left her both sick and impoverished.

The Christian response to the charging of fees for health care is clear in Matt 10:8: "Cure the sick, raise the dead, cleanse the lepers, cast out demons. You received without payment; give without payment." This prohibition against fees would have been a great attraction for patients, rich or poor, who might have been charged exorbitant fees by Greco-Roman physicians.

One story that may seem to contradict this notion of costless health care in Christianity is found in Mark 1:40–44, where a leper asks Jesus to cleanse him. Jesus instructs him, "See that you say nothing to anyone; but go, show yourself to the priest, and offer for your cleansing what Moses commanded, as a testimony to them" (v. 44). Jesus refers here to thanksgiving offerings outlined for "lepers" in Lev 14:1–32. These could be expensive but were graduated to the patient's income. Mark 1:44 makes clear, however, that Jesus' instruction was unique and was meant "as a testimony to them." Moreover, such an instruction would be moot after 70 C.E., when the temple no longer existed.

Despite the instruction in Mark 1:44, it is clear that the instruction in Matt 10:8 was interpreted to be normative insofar as fees were concerned. Indeed, there is evidence that the general sentiments reflected in Matthew against fees in Greco-Roman traditions continued into the second and third centuries. Tertullian, for example, apparently enjoys telling how Asclepius was punished with a thunderbolt "on the score of his avarice, because he made improper use of his healing skill."[19] The *Didache*, a document usually dated to the second century, warns against any Christian prophets who say "give me money, or something else."[20]

The fact that this animosity toward fees was seen as an advantage of early Christianity over other health care systems is advertised by Irenaeus in *Against Heresies* when speaking of the miracles done by the church: "She [the church] exerts day by day for the benefit of the Gentiles, neither practicing deception upon any, nor taking any reward from them."[21] Tertullian also notes that, in general, there are no fees for entrance into the Christian temple: "Even if there is a chest of a sort, it is not made up of money paid in entrance fees, as if religion were a matter of contract."[22]

To summarize, sentiments against fees expressed by New Testament writers continued into the second and third centuries and formed a coherent argument, among at least some apologists, on behalf of Christian health practices and against the practices of many Greco-Roman traditions. It is reasonable to conclude that many poor patients, and perhaps even wealthy ones, might be attracted to a system of health care that did not charge any fees. Even if Christian healers were no more efficacious than non-Christian ones, at least the patient would not lose any money.

CHAPTER SEVEN

Geographical Accessibility

As mentioned, where health care is dispensed is an important factor in the options that patients select, and in geographical accessibility, two types of resources may be distinguished: immobile and mobile. Christianity had a particular constellation of features that addressed the problems found with the mobile and immobile health care resources found in the Mediterranean world (see below). In essence, this chapter develops Ramsey MacMullen's acute observation that the most opportune place for conversion was perhaps "the room of some sick person."[1]

IMMOBILE RESOURCES

Immobile resources for the sick in the Greco-Roman world consisted principally of *tabernae medicae,* temples, and water sources. We will not concentrate here on the so-called *valetudinarium,* a sort of hospital found in military installations. Such facilities (e.g., that in Vetera on the lower Rhine, active during the time of Nero) were mostly found in the frontiers rather than in Rome or other cities in Italy, and were not available for most people.

Many towns had *tabernae medicae*—akin to street-side shops—where surgery and other medical assistance could be provided.[2] Examples have been found at Pompeii and other sites. The problem with these establishments, aside from the fees charged, was that they were not numerous. In addition, some of these physician's "clinics" or houses were located on hilly ground, which could be difficult to traverse, as is the case with the so-called House of the Surgeon in Pompeii.[3]

The Romans were particularly famous for the construction and promotion of therapeutic baths. According to one estimate, about 17 percent of the water supply in Rome was allotted to baths.[4] Not all baths, however, were equal in the number or types of diseases that they could service. Pliny the Elder, for example, says that the spring at Thespiae caused women to conceive. The water of Lake Alphius "removes psoriasis."[5] A spring in Gaul cures bladder stones.[6] Such specialization, however, meant that no one water source could serve the needs of all the sick. This could pose difficulties for those who did not live near the water source that was suitable for their illness.

Israelite religion also deemed water significant in healing. The most famous case, the story of Naaman (2 Kings 5), dating perhaps to a preexilic tradition, probably involves the use of the river Jordan to cure leprosy. Josephus's *Jewish Antiquities* mentions that Herod's search for a cure took him to the warm baths at Callirrhoe, near the Jordan.[7] Also near the Jordan, a mass grave (ca. 614 C.E.) apparently contains the remains of sick visitors in search of healing in the famous waters. Thus, the Jordan and its associated waters may have been used for healing from preexilic times through the early Christian period.

Ritual-bath installations called miqvā'ōt (sing. miqveh), dating from the Second Commonwealth on, have been uncovered in many Jewish communities (e.g., the Jewish quarter in Jerusalem, Masada), but they probably were not used for normal therapeutic reasons.[8] Near the Sea of Galilee, the large thermal-bath complex that thrived from the second century to the end of the first millennium at Hammath Gader is explicitly associated in inscriptions with therapy and may have been used by Romans, Christians, Jews, and Muslims.[9]

The most obvious immobile healing resources were temples, and major cities usually had at least one temple devoted to a healing deity. The most famous were probably those dedicated to Asclepius. The temples of Asclepius were often specifically designed for the sick. As the Edelsteins note, "In ground plan and construction the Asclepius sanctuaries seemed not to have differed from those of other divinities, with the exception of two features: the Asclepieia had buildings attached to them which were intended to house the patients and to provide the necessary means for their treatment; besides, there was the hall in which the patients slept."[10] Pausanias says that within the precincts of the Asclepieion near a place called Tithorea were dwellings for both the suppliants and the temple servants.[11]

Pausanias also notes that some of the sanctuaries were placed on roads well suited for carriages.[12]

Difficulty of access, however, was still evident in many ancient sources. While some of the famous Asclepieia were comfortable and accessible, it is likely that the vast majority were located in places that were difficult for the sick to navigate. Even in some large cities Asclepieia could be situated in relatively inaccessible locations. Strabo, for example, notes that the shrine of Asclepius at Carthage was situated on a "fairly steep height."[13]

Complaints about having to travel to Asclepieia appear in a remarkable passage in Themistius (fourth century C.E.): "If we were ill in body and required the help of the god, and he was present here in the temple and the acropolis, and were offering himself to the sick, just as even of old he is said to have done, would it be necessary to go to Tricca and sail to Epidauros on account of their ancient fame, or to move two steps and get rid of our illness?"[14]

The Isis traditions certainly encouraged the visits to temples for healing. Some temples may have accommodated clients for long stays. Lucius, the unfortunate character in the *Metamorphoses,* says that he established a dwelling there.[15] But the temples of Isis were not necessarily convenient for patients. The Iseum Campense at Rome, for example, was not easy to navigate. Turcan notes, "To attend the services one had to go round the edifice, passing through a long forecourt opposite the temple."[16] Along the way were stairs and other inconvenient obstacles.[17] In addition to all these hindrances in the sanctuary were those the patient probably encountered on the way to the Iseum.

Even more troublesome were assaults from highway bandits. Banditry was a highly common threat in Greco-Roman times.[18] Herod the Great spent much time, and acquired much glory, for his efforts against brigands.[19] Banditry could deter patients from venturing to distant shrines. Libanius, for example, notes how "the outrages of the district send away uncured" multitudes of those who come to the shrines of Asclepius in Cilicia.[20] Although it may not be typical, there is also a patient's report (141 B.C.E.) of being beaten at a place called Kerkeorisis: "While I was staying at the great Iseum here for a cure because of the illness which encompassed me, the minister Horus beat me with his rod."[21]

Jewish traditions were a bit different for immobile resources. Therapy was usually not allowed to take place in the temple. Furthermore, as noted, in the more stringent forms of Judaism, there was really only one temple. Thus, even if the temple offered therapeutic services, most people would need to travel long distances to reach the site. The allowance of only one temple may have helped encourage in Judaism the idea of healing at a distance. This notion is evinced most clearly in 1 Kgs 8:37–39, which is part of the so-called Prayer of Solomon:

> If there is famine in the land, . . . whatever plague, whatever sickness there is; whatever prayer, whatever plea there is from any individual or from all your people Israel, all knowing the afflictions of their own hearts so that they stretch out their hands toward this house; then hear in heaven your dwelling place.

In effect, the author is advertising that it is not necessary to come to the temple to receive healing. Simply extending the hands toward the temple was sufficient to receive healing, no matter the distance; the temple could function as a long-distance therapeutic device.

In sum, the problems with immobile resources were significant for patients. The most famous places could be quite a distance from a patient's home. Travelers incurred costs, and there was a real danger of being assaulted. The most celebrated places were also crowded. For example, Strabo notes that the temple of Asclepius at Epidaurus was "always full of the sick."[22] Thus, even if one could get to Epidaurus, there was no guarantee of being treated.

Christianity addresses the problem of immobile and centralized therapeutic centers dramatically in the story of the paralytic in John 5:2–9:

> Now in Jerusalem by the Sheep Gate there is a pool, called in Hebrew Beth-zatha, which has five porticoes. In these lay many invalids— blind, lame, and paralyzed. One man was there who had been ill for thirty-eight years. When Jesus saw him lying there and knew that he had been there a long time, he said to him, "Do you want to be made well?" The sick man answered him, "Sir, I have no one to put me into the pool when the water is stirred up; and while I am making my way, someone else steps down ahead of me." Jesus said to him, "Stand up, take your mat and walk." At once the man was made well, and he took up his mat and began to walk. Now that day was a Sabbath.

The story shows plainly that one of the problems with this pool was that traveling to it could be difficult for those with physical challenges. The story also notes that this place was crowded, rendering it difficult for a patient to benefit from the locus even if he or she succeeded in arriving there. The biblical author emphasizes that the patient "had been there a long time." All of these problems with immobile therapeutic loci, though they may have literary motives in the Bible, echo Greco-Roman literature.

The solution proposed by Jesus is not to disperse the crowd or retrieve water from the pool for the man. Instead, the solution is astoundingly simple. Jesus instructs the man to "stand up, take your mat and walk." Such a story means that going to a distant, crowded, and otherwise inconvenient therapeutic center was not necessary.

Early Christian texts show that healing at a distance, like that which occurred in 1 Kings 8, was emphasized even more by Christianity. The story of the centurion's servant in Matt 8:5–10 illustrates the high value of such healing:

> When he entered Capernaum, a centurion came to him, appealing to him and saying, "Lord, my servant is lying at home paralyzed, in terrible distress." And he said to him, "I will come and cure him." The centurion answered, "Lord, I am not worthy to have you come under my roof; but only speak the word, and my servant will be healed. For I also am a man under authority, with soldiers under me; and I say to one, 'Go,' and he goes, and to another, 'Come,' and he comes, and to my slave, 'Do this,' and the slave does it." When Jesus heard him, he was amazed and said to those who followed him, "Truly I tell you, in no one in Israel have I found such faith."

No longer does a patient need to be brought to a healing center. A healer need not even be where the patient is. Geography poses no obstacle to faith.

This concept supersedes and enhances the notion of praying toward the temple in 1 Kings 8. Indeed, the issue of praying toward a temple became moot after the destruction of the temple in 70 C.E. Thus, Christianity, which has no temple per se, seems to have provided a most attractive solution to the problem of geography and health care. Crowded, distant, and expensive therapeutic loci were theoretically eliminated altogether. Faith, not a temple or any therapeutic locus, was virtually the only requirement in this Christian health care system.

MOBILE RESOURCES

Mobile resources consist, for the most part, of consultants who visited the sick in their homes or other places where the patients might be. Mobile consultants are usually attractive to patients simply because of the sheer convenience of not having to travel with an illness. In his *Life* (403–404), Josephus relates how he was taken to Capernaum after falling off a horse in battle. Physicians, presumably local, were summoned, and he was treated for a day. As noted, most Greco-Roman medical literature assumes that visiting the homes of the sick was a normal practice for physicians. Still, the mobility of such itinerant physicians also offered serious problems for patients. It cannot be presumed that the type of mobile service offered by physicians to Josephus was always available for more common citizens. Galen, for example, notes that some physicians "have become so extremely overcome by laziness that they do not visit patients, many of whom live nearby."[23] The unpredictable schedule of these consultants may also have been a problem.

Perhaps the most significant problem with itinerant healers was that one could never be sure of their quality. Roaming physicians were disparaged by Galen, who regarded their wandering as a license to escape their poor reputation:[24] "A wanderer who visits many places has no right except to be called an impostor with a (special) skill in this matter."[25] Galen's treatise foregrounds the fact that there was no empirewide accreditation system for physicians. Clearly, therefore, while mobile consultants provided many conveniences, some method of accreditation was needed in the first and second centuries.

Christianity also focused on providing mobile consultants. The paradigmatic statement on the obligation of Christians to travel to the sick is in Matt 10:8: "Cure the sick, raise the dead, cleanse the lepers, cast out demons. You received without payment; give without payment." As Crossan notes, the fact that *Gospel of Thomas* 14.2 contains a parallel instruction to go heal the sick strongly attests to the antiquity of this tradition.[26] Many New Testament scholars argue that Jesus' itinerant healing practices reflected the adoption of a Cynic lifestyle, which also emphasized wandering. Christianity, however, may have been simply continuing practices that were known in other healing traditions, such as discussed above.[27]

Perhaps we may see Christianity as a Jewish sect that was concerned with broadening the parameters of health care offered under traditional Judaism. Christians were to provide health care to Jews as well as Gentiles. This broadening of the geo-ethnic parameters may even reach back to the historical Jesus. Franz Annen, in his exhaustive study of the tradition of Jesus' healings of the Gadarene demoniacs, concludes, "Jesus certainly worked as an exorcist, most probably even outside of Jewish territory and among gentiles."[28]

Even if Christianity eliminated the need for centralized thera-peutic loci, many non-Christian patients needed to be reached. Chris-tianity, after all, was targeting non-Christian patients as part of its missionary strategy. As late as the third century, evidence indicates that Christians continued this practice. Dionysius of Alexandria, in his *Epistle to the Alexandrians,* mentions that many Christian brethren "visited the sick."[29] Indeed, in areas where healers may not have been abundant, mobile healers were probably quite welcome among non-Christians who may not have had other options.

Still, the problems mentioned by Galen concerning the certifi-cation of healers would not have disappeared with the mere advent of Christian mobile healers. Evidence suggests that Christianity sought to provide methods by which the problems in certifying healers could be ameliorated or eliminated altogether. Some of these problems and Christian solutions are encapsulated in Acts 19:13–20, the story of the seven sons of Sceva, the Jewish priest:

> Then some itinerant Jewish exorcists tried to use the name of the Lord Jesus over those who had evil spirits, saying, "I adjure you by the Jesus whom Paul proclaims." Seven sons of a Jewish high priest named Sceva were doing this. But the evil spirit said to them in reply, "Jesus I know, and Paul I know; but who are you?" Then the man with the evil spirit leaped on them, mastered them all, and so overpowered them that they fled out of the house naked and wounded. When this became known to all residents of Ephesus, both Jews and Greeks, everyone was awestruck; and the name of the Lord Jesus was praised. Also many of those who became believers confessed and disclosed their practices. A number of those who practiced magic collected their books and burned them publicly; when the value of these books was calculated, it was found to come to fifty thousand silver coins. So the word of the Lord grew mightily and prevailed.

The story centers on wandering Jewish healers (v. 13: τινες καὶ τῶν περιερχομένων 'Ιουδαίων) who apparently competed with Christian healers. According to the author of Acts, the reputation of Christian healers was such that these wandering healers sought to imi-tate them.

The author of the story seems worried about the very concern Galen had in mind when dealing with itinerant healers: how do pa-tients know that they are interacting with reputable healers? The au-thor wanted to help patients identify the genuine Christian healer from the fraudulent. Apparently some itinerant healers sought to cap-italize on the Christian healing reputation, and they might have been creating a problem. According to the author of Acts, true Christian healers could not be identified merely by their use of the name Jesus. Rather, they had to have a proper relationship with Jesus and, by implication, with the followers of Paul. Indeed, the demon declares that "he knows Paul." Thus, affiliation with the proper group, and not merely the use of the simple Christian techniques, was necessary. Such healers must have the imprimatur of Paul or of other recognized Christians.

Equally important in identifying a reputable healer is that the genuine Christian healer could be identified by the lack of fees, by the disinterest in fees. The sheer economic attraction of not charging fees has been explored above. As noted, Matt 10:8 was perhaps a paradigmatic statement about fees. In Acts 8:20, Peter's reply to Simon, who had sought to buy the power he saw in apostles, summarizes this sentiment against fees: "May your silver perish with you, because you thought you could obtain God's gift with money!"

Christians in the second and even third centuries continued to use the trademarks of Christian healers encouraged in the New Testament. Galen, for instance, confirms that Christians had sufficient trademarks to be compared to a school.[30] Even into the third century, Cyprian mentions that some people call Christians "Clinics" because of their medical practices.[31] The *Didache* says that if a prophet "ask for money, he is a false prophet."[32] This shows that some Christian communities were establishing standards to identify genuine itinerant Christian healers from fraudulent ones.

SUMMARY

New Testament writers seem to have been familiar with the problems geography posed to health care access. They knew that centralized therapeutic loci could be crowded and difficult for the physically challenged to approach. Christianity, as portrayed in the New Testament, eliminated the need for centralized therapeutic loci altogether. Faith transcended the need for any single therapeutic locus. Among Greco-Romans, this would have eliminated the need to travel to expensive, crowded, and distant places. Among many Jews, this would have replaced the idea of praying toward a temple that no longer existed after 70 C.E. Faith did not, however, eliminate the need for Christian healers to travel to sick patients. Traveling to the sick was still part of the Christian missionary agenda, which combined health care reform with an effort to bring the kingdom of God to fruition.

The certification of itinerant healers was a widespread problem that Christianity sought to neutralize by providing a sort of "franchise" or "brand-name" approach, insofar as certain affiliations and practices signaled reputability. Such "franchise" approaches may be seen in the number of Greco-Roman healers who claimed to be affiliated with the traditions of Hippocrates and other famous physicians. The significant Christian innovation—its trademark—however, was that no fees would be demanded of patients. Thus, all things being equal in therapeutic efficacy, the lack of fees would eliminate the largest complaint related by Greco-Roman writers such as Galen: the danger of losing money to itinerant healers. Even if Christian healers were not effective, the patient would not have to worry about this aspect of itinerant health care.

CHAPTER EIGHT

Time

JEWISH AND GRECO-ROMAN TRADITIONS

Temporal restrictions might affect when a patient could receive health care. These restrictions can range from specific religious prohibitions against administering health care on certain days to the amount of time that a pool of consultants had available for patients. A patient's available time could also influence the strategy for seeking health care.

As noted, while the Hebrew Bible bore many rules that affected when health care could be administered, it contained no direct discussion about healing on the Sabbath. Jewish literature from the late Second Temple period, however, corroborates the existence of restrictions on the days when health care could be administered. For example, CD 11:16–17 has the following discussion on what is not permitted on the Sabbath: "And any living man who falls into a place of water or into a place. . . . No one should take him out with a ladder or a rope or a utensil."[1]

Lawrence Schiffman argues that this passage should not be seen as a prohibition against any means to save the man in the well, because this would be "antithetical to the spirit of Judaism."[2] His reason seems to be a theological, not a historical, judgment. It assumes that the author(s) of the *Damascus Document* did not intend to be antithetical to the forms of Judaism that Schiffman regards as providing the representative spirit of Judaism. Were we to apply this criterion to the stream of Judaism that became known as Christianity, then nothing in this form of Judaism could be interpreted to be antithetical to the spirit of Judaism.

Schiffman defends his view by alluding to the Serekh-Damascus scroll (4Q265 [4QSD]), the relevant portion of which he translates, "And if it is a human being who falls in[to] the water on the Sabbath [day,] he (the rescuer) should extend to him his garment to bring him up with it, but he should not pick up an instrument."[3]

Schiffman argues that the passage in the *Damascus Document* refers to the avoidance, "if possible," of some utensils. He claims that if one could not save a life without the forbidden utensils, then we should infer that those utensils would be permitted. But here he goes beyond what is stated in the text of these documents. They never say to avoid these utensils "if possible"; therefore, we should assume, unless there is contrary evidence, that the authors meant what they said.

Such restrictions against saving a life on the Sabbath probably existed in the Jewish communities of the first century in at least part of the Mediterranean basin. The question posed to Jesus in Matt 12:10 ("Is it lawful to cure on the sabbath?"), which alludes to the example of a sheep that has fallen into a well, certainly assumes a negative answer. It is reasonable, then, to assume that at least some forms of Judaism in the first century regarded healing as a type of work that was not lawful on the Sabbath, even if this meant denying lifesaving measures.[4]

Temporal restrictions and preferences were not limited to certain forms of Judaism. Some secular Greco-Roman traditions also had preferences about the proper time for healing. Speaking of the proper length of time for a diagnosis, Galen notes a "customary three-day period of delay according to many physicians who follow Thessalus and others. They insist on keeping up this custom as if it is a revelation from God."[5] In addition, the temples of Asclepius were not always open, and priests were sometimes busy with other chores. This was particularly the case in small towns. Moreover, the god was not always available, as he was believed to take "vacations" or trips. In *The Rich Man*, one of Aristophanes' satirical plays, a woman complains of her experience at a temple of Asclepius: "Has good news arrived? For I've been sitting waiting till I'm tired within. Waiting for him [Asclepius] and longing for good news."[6] Waiting for Asclepius could be recognized as a problem that was sufficiently significant to attract a satirist such as Aristophanes.

In addition, illnesses and mortality rates varied seasonally much more than they do today. The advent of antibiotics and modern technology has leveled such variations. One of the most extensive studies of the seasonal nature of illnesses is that of Brent Shaw, who studied the death commemorations of nearly four thousand persons in Rome in the middle of the first millennium. The findings concerning seasonality probably are valid for the first century as well.[7]

The general results of Shaw's study were that deaths among adults (twenty to forty-nine years of age) rose sharply in the late summer and early fall (August-October). In May, for example, Shaw's sample listed approximately eighty deaths, but this rose to nearly two hundred deaths in September. Since approximately 94 percent of the selected inscriptions indicated the gender of the deceased, Shaw was able to conclude that the peak of deaths for women seems to have come slightly earlier in the summer than for men.[8] The elderly, defined as those over fifty to sixty years of age, experienced two critical periods, one in the winter months and the other in September. Shaw concludes that "the winter months represent an ever-increasing share of all deaths with each succeeding aging cohort."[9] He also suggests that the countryside was healthier than an urban metropolis for the reasons already discussed (e.g., higher population densities increase the incidence of infectious diseases).

The implications of such studies for the temporal aspects of health care delivery are significant. At the peak of certain ailments, physicians may not have had the time to treat as many patients as in the low seasons of illness. If physicians migrated to cities in the expectation of more patients, then there might have been a greater imbalance created in other areas. L. Cohn-Haft concludes, "For better or worse, the secular physicians produced by apprenticeship and the schools were all the Hellenistic world had, and the weight of the evidence indicates an insufficient number of such trained doctors to meet the need for their services."[10]

CHRISTIANITY

Christianity responded to the issue of temporal restrictions in a number of ways. Perhaps the most significant was the abolition of legal temporal restrictions altogether, as illustrated in Matt 12:9–15:

> He [Jesus] left that place and entered their synagogue; a man was there with a withered hand, and they asked him, "Is it lawful to cure on the sabbath?" so that they might accuse him. He said to them, "Suppose one of you has only one sheep and it falls into a pit on the sabbath; will

you not lay hold of it and lift it out? How much more valuable is a human being than a sheep! So it is lawful to do good on the sabbath." Then he said to the man, "Stretch out your hand." He stretched it out, and it was restored, as sound as the other. But the Pharisees went out and conspired against him, how to destroy him. When Jesus became aware of this, he departed. Many crowds followed him, and he cured all of them.

This pericope has at least two significant features for our purposes. First, as noted above, the author presumes that there was a prohibition against healing on the Sabbath, something corroborated by the *Damascus Document* mentioned above. Second, the story clearly opposes this health care policy. By setting the confrontation in a synagogue the author seems to emphasize that Jesus was critiquing at least some traditional forms of Judaism.

Christianity's answer, as depicted in Jesus' actions in this story, was to abolish temporal restrictions altogether. There was no day of the week in which health care could not be administered. Moreover, a principle was also enunciated: restoring human health took precedence over rules about time. Finally, the notion of simple prayer and faith, which did not require work as defined by Jewish law, rendered moot all temporal restrictions on healing. Christianity may be seen as a Jewish sect that had, as one primary goal, the reformation of the health care system enunciated by the forms of Judaism that held Leviticus to be normative.

Equally significant, Christianity abolished temporal restrictions current in Greco-Roman traditions. For example, diagnosis was either immediate or insignificant in Christianity. Christian healers would not wait the three days mentioned by Galen to make a diagnosis. Therapy was also immediate. This feature of the Christian health care system would have been attractive to patients seeking immediate relief from their suffering. Even if Christian therapy was no more medically effective than that of other traditions, at least the immediate attention paid to a patient's problem, even on the Sabbath, offered a type of relief not found elsewhere.

CHAPTER NINE

Comparative Synthesis

The healing stories in the New Testament were more than literary devices meant to promote Jesus' power and the announcement of the kingdom of God. They evince awareness of the problems of health care that were voiced throughout the Greco-Roman world. These ranged from the cost of health care to access to therapeutic loci. The New Testament authors of healing stories likewise knew that Christian health care ideas were a primary means to gain new converts. It may be no accident that so many of the stories portray converts coming to Jesus for answers to their health care problems rather than for answers to some cosmic, political, or eschatological question.

Perhaps the most significant aspect of Christianity, as evinced in the New Testament, is that it simplified health care from what was being offered by other forms of Judaism and Greco-Roman traditions. In the late Second Temple period, many other streams of Judaism were growing in therapeutic complexity because of an increasingly complex angelology. Likewise, many Greco-Roman traditions had complex therapeutic ritual structures. Christianity simplified therapy by emphasizing the sufficiency of faith and the name of Jesus. Despite an etiological system that assumed as many demons as in Judaism, Christianity's therapeutic ritual structure was simplified by its emphasis on Jesus as the cure.

This emphasis on faith also neutralized the problems of geographical access to health care. Many Greco-Roman healing temples were distant. Water sources were sometimes so specialized that matching a water source with a patient's illness could mean traveling to a distant area. Therapeutic loci could also be crowded and expensive because of the cost of the petitionary, therapeutic, or thanksgiving rituals. Faith, in contrast, could work at a distance.

Christianity also may be seen as a Jewish sect that sought to redefine the socioreligious status of the patient. The Levitical health care system excluded chronically ill patients from the community and so ruptured the Jewish community. Its policies had, in effect, rendered the chronically ill a discrete and identifiable demographic group that must have gained significant numbers by the first century. Christianity opposed the Levitical health care system by redefining purity in a manner akin to the Asclepian tradition. Purity of thought, not of body, became primary. This may have been part of an innovative effort to reunite the Israelite "family."

Likewise, Christianity eliminated all temporal restrictions on health care found in other forms of Judaism. Christians administered health care on the Sabbath or any other day of the week. But Christianity also neutralized temporal restrictions found in Greco-Roman traditions, some of which created delays in the administration of both diagnosis and therapy. Seasonal fluctuations in the incidence of disease also may have affected the time that physicians had available for patients. In Christianity all diagnosis and therapy became immediate.

Equally significant is the elimination of all fees in Christian health care. Fees were perhaps the most common characteristic of both religious and secular Greco-Roman traditions. The temples of Asclepius could demand expensive thanksgiving offerings. Secular physicians might demand exorbitant fees. Christianity not only sought to render health care affordable but also helped to neutralize one of the most recurrent complaints about healers in the Greco-Roman world: the vulnerability of patients to unscrupulous, unqualified, and greedy health care practitioners. Regardless of the efficacy of Christian therapeutic practices, the lack of fees rendered Christian healing most attractive to many patients who had no other resort.

The elimination of fees also meant that Christian mobile healers were rendered much less suspect. Itinerancy was part of the Christian mission as well as a necessary health care practice for those who did not have facile access to therapeutic loci or the most reputable physicians. Regardless of the efficacy of Christian healing, patients were guaranteed no further economic loss by consulting Christian healers.

This study has intentionally avoided the issue of the extent to which these ideas about health care reach back to the historical Jesus. In many respects this question is not answerable on the basis of present data. We can only speculate that the historical Jesus perhaps had the reformation of health care as a principal part of his agenda. Meier,

Crossan, and other scholars seem to agree that healing activities formed an authentic memory about Jesus. Perhaps further research about Galilee may reveal that it was sufficiently removed from the central powers at Jerusalem to begin a reformation in health care.

The early Christian approach to health care did not last long; it eventually became complex as well. By the late third and the fourth centuries, conventional health care had become prevalent. The notion that illness was a welcome human experience was yet another way to confront the intractability and lack of efficacy of any sort of health care. It reflects a resignation to the fact that Christianity could not eradicate illness or even deal with it more efficaciously than any other health care system.[1]

Nevertheless, early Christianity may be seen as a Jewish sect that had, as one of its primary goals, the reformation of the health care systems of stricter forms of Judaism and sought to address other problems found in the health care systems of Greco-Roman traditions. Far from being a marginal interest, health care was part of the core of its mission and strategy for gaining converts to this Jewish sect. A variety of features afforded Christianity an advantage over its many competitors (see synopsis chart). The combination of benefits offered by the Christian approach to health care was one of the primary factors in the rise of Christianity.

Synopsis of the Main Features of Selected Health Care Systems in the Eastern Mediterranean (ca. first and second centuries C.E.)

Features	Tradition				
	Asclepius	Isis	Secular Greco-Roman	Levitical	Christian
Illness unrelated to patient's social or religious status	Yes	No	No	No	Yes
Simple therapeutic ritual structure	No	No	No	N/A	Yes
Sufficiency of faith/prayer for healing	No	No	No	No	Yes
Free health care	No	No	No	No	Yes
Location of patient has no effect on care	No	No	No	No	Yes
Mobile consultants	Yes	N/A	Yes	N/A	Yes
Lack of temporal restrictions	No	No	No	No	Yes

Notes

NOTES TO INTRODUCTION (pages 1–15)

[1] Biographical material on Atkinson is based on Peggy Humphrey, *María Atkinson—la Madre de México: No Doubt Here* (Cleveland, Tenn.: Pathway, 1967).

[2] Unless noted otherwise, all English quotations of the Bible are from the NRSV.

[3] See Morton Kelsey, *Healing and Christianity* (Minneapolis: Augsburg, 1995), 44–45.

[4] For a recent treatment of the literary motives of some healing stories, see S. J. Roth, *The Blind, the Lame, and the Poor: Character Types in Luke–Acts* (Sheffield: Sheffield Academic Press, 1997).

[5] On the correlation of these plagues with the introduction of Asclepius, see Ludwig Edelstein and Emma Edelstein, *Asclepius* (2 vols.; Baltimore: Johns Hopkins University Press, 1945).

[6] R. E. Witt, *Isis in the Ancient World* (Baltimore: Johns Hopkins University Press, 1997), 236.

[7] See John E. Stambaugh, *The Ancient Roman City* (Baltimore: Johns Hopkins University Press, 1988).

[8] See, e.g., F. L. Black, "Measles Endemicity in Insular Populations: Critical Community Size and Its Evolutionary Implications," *Journal of Theoretical Biology* 11 (1966): 207–11; and T. Aidan Cockburn, "Infectious Diseases in Ancient Populations," *Current Anthropology* 12 (1971): 51–56.

[9] William H. McNeill, *Plagues and Peoples* (New York: Doubleday, 1976), 53.

[10] Colin Wells, *The Roman Empire* (2d ed.; Cambridge: Harvard University Press, 1992), 88.

[11] Ralph Jackson, *Doctors and Diseases in the Roman Empire* (Norman: University of Oklahoma Press, 1988), 173.

[12] See Donald Engels, *Roman Corinth* (Chicago: University of Chicago Press, 1990), 28, 84

[13] L. Michael White, "Urban Development and Social Change in Imperial Ephesos," in *Ephesos: Metropolis of Asia* (ed. Helmut Koester; Valley Forge, Penn.: Trinity Press International, 1995), 35.

[14] For a general treatment of the role of nutrition in world history, see Robert I. Rotberg and Theodore K. Rabb, *Hunger and History: The Impact of Changing Food Production and Consumption Patterns of Society* (Cambridge: Cambridge University Press, 1985).

[15] Peter Richardson, *Herod: King of the Jews and Friend of the Romans* (Columbia: University of South Carolina Press, 1996), 222–23.

[16] See Wells, *The Roman Empire*, 88.

[17] Pliny the Elder, *Natural History* 26.1.

[18] See George Kohn, "Antonine Plague (Plague of Galen)," in *Encyclopedia of Plague and Pestilence* (New York: Facts on File, 1995), 6–7.

[19] Stevan L. Davies, *Jesus the Healer: Possession Trance and the Origins of Christianity* (New York: Continuum, 1995), 15.

[20] Eldon J. Epp and George W. MacRae, eds., *The New Testament and Its Modern Interpreters* (Philadelphia: Fortress, 1989).

[21] Darrel W. Amundsen, *Medicine, Society, and Faith in the Ancient and Medieval Worlds* (Baltimore: Johns Hopkins University Press, 1996), 9.

[22] Gary B. Ferngren, "Early Christianity As a Religion of Healing," *Bulletin of the History of Medicine* 66 (1992): 1–15.

[23] See, e.g., Vivian Nutton, "Medicine in Late Antiquity and the Middle Ages," in *The Western Medical Tradition, 800 BC to AD 1800* (ed. Lawrence Conrad et al.; Cambridge: Cambridge University Press, 1995), 71–91.

[24] J. D. Crossan, *The Historical Jesus: The Life of a Jewish Mediterranean Peasant* (New York: Harper & Row, 1991), 422

[25] John P. Meier, *A Marginal Jew: Rethinking the Historical Jesus* (2 vols.; New York: Doubleday, 1991–1994), 2:726.

[26] The criterion of embarrassment, which is widely used in modern New Testament scholarship (e.g., ibid., 1:68–71), asserts that one may regard a tradition about the historical Jesus as authentic if it is preserved despite the embarrassment it could cause. The presupposition is that such an embarrassing tradition was so well known that it was better to explain it than to eliminate it altogether.

[27] Rodney Stark, *The Rise of Christianity: A Sociologist Reconsiders History* (Princeton: Princeton University Press, 1996).

[28] Adolf von Harnack, "Medicinisches aus der ältesten Kirchengeschichte," TUGAL 8 (4, 1892): 37–152.

[29] Ibid., 132: "Das Christentum ist medicinische Religion: das ist seine Stärke, in manchen Ausgestaltungen auch seine Schwäche."

[30] Brief allusions to such competition may be seen in Vivian Nutton, "Murders and Miracles: Lay Attitudes towards Medicine in Classical Antiquity," in *Patients and Practitioners: Lay Perceptions of Medicine in Pre-*

industrial Society (ed. Roy Porter; Cambridge: Cambridge University Press, 1985), 23–53.

[31] Bernd Kollmann, *Jesus und die Christen als Wundertäter: Studien, Medizin, und Schamanismus in Antike und Christentum* (Göttingen: Vandenhoeck & Ruprecht, 1996).

[32] Dieter Lührmann, "Neutestamentliche Wundergeschichten und antike Medizin," in *Religious Propaganda and Missionary Competition in the New Testament World* (ed. Lukas Borman, Kelly Del Tredici, and Angela Standharatinger; Leiden: E. J. Brill, 1994), 198: "Ein solcher kurzer und notwendig verkürzender Überblick über die Forschung zu den neutestamentlichen Wundergeschichten zeigt, dass der Vergleich mit antiker Medizin bisher kein Rolle gespielt hat."

[33] Evelyn Frost, *Christian Healing: A Consideration of the Place of Spiritual Healing in the Church of Today in the Light of the Ante-Nicene Church* (London: A. R. Mowbray & Co., 1949).

[34] A similar argument is made by Ronald Kydd, "Jesus, Saints, and Relics: Approaching the Early Church through Healing," *Journal of Pentecostal Theology* 2 (1993): 91–104.

[35] Examples of sociological approaches include Bruce J. Malina, *Christian Origins and Cultural Anthropology* (Atlanta: John Knox, 1986); Gerd Theissen, *Sociology of Early Palestinian Christianity* (trans. John Bowden; Philadelphia: Fortress, 1978). For a medical-anthropological approach to Near Eastern health care systems, see Hector Avalos, *Illness and Health Care in the Ancient Near East: The Role of the Temple in Greece, Mesopotamia, and Israel* (HSM 54; Atlanta: Scholars Press, 1995); and "Medicine," *OEANE* 3:450–59. For a combination of a sociological and feminist approach to the study of illness, see Carole Fontaine, "Disabilities and Illness in the Bible: A Feminist Perspective," in *A Feminist Companion to the Hebrew Bible in the New Testament* (ed. Athalya Brenner; Sheffield: Sheffield Academic Press, 1996), 286–300.

[36] Among the most important studies by John J. Pilch are "Sickness and Healing in Luke–Acts," in *The Social World of Luke–Acts* (ed. Jerome Neyrey; Peabody, Mass.: Hendrickson, 1991), 181–209; "The Health Care System in Matthew: A Social Science Analysis," *BTB* 16 (3, 1986): 281–83; "Healing in Mark: A Social Science Analysis," *BTB* 15 (4, 1985): 142–50; "Biblical Leprosy and Body Symbolism," *BTB* 11 (4, 1981): 108–13.

[37] Pilch was also a prime organizer of a 1993 Society of Biblical Literature conference on medical anthropology and the historical Jesus. See Eugene H. Lovering, ed., *SBL Seminar Papers, 1993* (SBLSP 30; Atlanta: Scholars Press, 1993).

[38] For a brief survey of some debates within anthropology on Douglas's theories, see Brian Morris, *Anthropological Studies of Religion: An Introductory Text* (Cambridge: Cambridge University Press, 1987), 226–32.

[39] See esp. Morton Smith, *Jesus the Magician* (San Francisco: Harper Collins, 1978).

[40] Susan R. Garrett, *The Demise of the Devil: Magic and the Demonic in Luke's Writings* (Minneapolis: Fortress, 1989), 23–26; and Graham H. Twelftree, *Jesus the Exorcist: A Contribution to the Study of the Historical Jesus* (Peabody, Mass.: Hendrickson, 1993), 190–207. For a recent discussion of Apollonius of Tyana, see Erkki Koskenniemi, "Apollonius of Tyana: A Typical θεῖος ἀνήρ?" *JBL* 117 (3, 1998): 455–67.

[41] Howard Clark Kee, *Medicine, Miracle, and Magic in New Testament Times* (Cambridge: Cambridge University Press, 1986).

[42] Ibid., 2.

[43] Ibid., 68–69.

[44] Twelftree, *Jesus the Exorcist*, 228.

[45] For a similar focus on exorcism, see Dieter Trunk, *Der messianische Heiler: Eine redaktions- und religionsgeschichtliche Studie zu den Exorzismen im Matthäusevangelium* (Freiberg: Herder, 1994). As the subtitle of his book indicates, however, Trunk, though very interested in comparing biblical materials with those of non-Christian religions in the Greco-Roman period, is primarily occupied with redaction and form criticism.

[46] Davies, *Jesus the Healer*, 171.

[47] Ibid., 119.

[48] Harold Remus, *Jesus As Healer* (Cambridge: Cambridge University Press, 1997); *Pagan-Christian Conflict over Miracle in the Second Century* (Cambridge, Mass.: Philadelphia Patristic Foundation, 1983). For a similar and more theologically oriented discussion of illness, see John Christopher Thomas, *The Devil, Disease, and Deliverance: Origins of Illness in New Testament Thought* (Sheffield: Sheffield Academic Press, 1998).

[49] Galen, *De optimo medico cognoscendo libelli versionem arabicam primum edidit, in linguam anglicam vertit, commentatus est Albert Z. Iskander* (ed. Albert Z. Iskander; Corpus medicorum graecorum supplementum orientale 4; Berlin: Akademie, 1988). See the important review by Vivian Nutton, "The Patient's Choice: A New Treatise by Galen," *CQ* 40 (1, 1990): 236–57.

[50] Brent D. Shaw, "Seasons of Death: Aspects of Mortality in Imperial Rome," *JRS* 86 (1996): 100–138.

[51] See, e.g., G. F. Moore, *Judaism in the First Centuries of the Christian Era: The Age of the Tannaim* (3 vols.; 1927–1930; repr. in 2 vols., Peabody, Mass.: Hendrickson, 1997). Recent treatments of Judaism in the early Christian era include those of Lester L. Grabbe, *Judaism from Cyrus to Hadrian* (2 vols.; Minneapolis: Fortress, 1992). A critique of Grabbe is found in Steve Mason, "The Study of Early Judaism: A Dialogue with Lester Grabbe," *JAOS* 118 (3, 1995): 463–72.

[52] For a review of these debates, see Günter Stemberger, *Jewish Contemporaries of Jesus: Pharisees, Sadducees, Essenes* (Minneapolis: Fortress, 1995); Anthony J. Saldarini, *Pharisees, Scribes, and Sadducees in Palestinian Society* (Wilmington, Del.: Glazier, 1988).

[53] See Jacob Neusner, *Rabbinic Literature and the New Testament: What We Cannot Show, We Do Not Know* (Valley Forge, Penn.: Trinity Press Inter-

national, 1994); Geza Vermes, "Methodology in the Study of Jewish Literature in the Graeco-Roman Period," *JJS* 36 (2, 1985): 145–57; Baruch M. Bokser, "Recent Developments in the Study of Judaism, 70–200 C.E.," *SecCen* 3 (1983): 1–68.

[54] The editio princeps is that of Elisha Qimron and John Strugnell, *Qumran Cave 4*. Vol. 5, *Miqṣat Maʿaśe Ha-Torah* (DJD 10; Oxford: Clarendon, 1994). See also John Kampen and Moshe J. Bernstein, eds., *Reading 4QMMT: New Perspectives on Qumran Law and History* (Atlanta: Scholars Press, 1996).

[55] Daniel R. Schwartz, "MMT, Josephus, and the Pharisees," in *Reading 4QMMT* (ed. Kampen and Bernstein), 67–80.

[56] For the numerous references in *Miqṣat Maʿaseh ha-Torah* to Levitical rules, see also Joseph M. Baumgarten, "The 'Halakah' in *Miqṣat Maʿaseh ha-Torah* (MMT)," *JAOS* 116 (3, 1996): 512–16.

[57] For a recent statement of the still dominant position, see James H. Charlesworth, *Jesus and the Dead Sea Scrolls: The Controversy Resolved* (New York: Doubleday, 1992).

[58] For the theory that the Dead Sea Scrolls should be primarily associated with the Sadducees, see Lawrence Schiffman, *Reclaiming the Dead Sea Scrolls* (New York: Doubleday, 1994).

[59] A foremost representative of the theory that Qumran should not be linked with the production of the Dead Sea Scrolls is Norman Golb, *Who Wrote the Dead Sea Scrolls? The Search for the Secret of Qumran* (New York: Scribners, 1996).

[60] See F. M. Cross and Esther Eshel, "The Missing Link," *BAR* 24 (2, 1998): 48–53, 69; and "Ostraca from Khirbet Qumran," *IEJ* 47 (3–4, 1997): 17–28. For a critique of Cross and Eshel's interpretation of the ostracon, see Ada Yardeni, "Breaking the Missing Link," *BAR* 24 (3, 1998): 44–47; and "A Draft of a Deed of an Ostracon from Khirbet Qumran," *IEJ* 47 (3–4, 1997): 233–37.

[61] Peter Hayman, "Monotheism—a Misused Word in Jewish Studies?" *JJS* 42 (1, 1991): 1–15.

[62] Joseph Naveh and Shaul Shaked, *Magic Spells and Formulae: Aramaic Incantations of Late Antiquity* (Jerusalem: Magnes, 1993), 31

[63] See Douglas R. Edwards and C. Thomas McCollough, *Archaeology and the Galilee: Texts and Contexts in the Graeco-Roman and Byzantine Periods* (Atlanta: Scholars Press, 1997).

[64] Eric Meyers, "Jesus in His Galilean Context," in Edwards and McCollough, *Archaeology and the Galilee*, 64.

[65] For wide-ranging discussions of the two-source hypothesis, see Arthur J. Bellizoni Jr., ed., *The Two Source Hypothesis: A Critical Appraisal* (Macon, Ga.: Mercer, 1985). For criticism of the two-source hypothesis, see Allan J. McNicol, ed., *Beyond the Q Impasse—Luke's Use of Matthew* (Valley Forge, Penn.: Trinity Press International, 1996); William R. Farmer, *New Synoptic Studies* (Macon, Ga.: Mercer, 1983).

[66] For a history of the Near East during the Roman period, see Fergus Millar, *The Roman Near East, 31 BC–AD 337* (Cambridge: Harvard University Press, 1993). For a history of the Roman Empire, see Wells, *The Roman Empire*. A basic review of the history of Judaism during the Roman Empire is found in Grabbe, *Judaism from Cyrus to Hadrian*.

NOTES TO CHAPTER 1 (pages 19–30)

[1] For further comments on the anthropological approach and biblical studies, see Bernhard Lang, ed., *Anthropological Approaches to the Old Testament* (Philadelphia: Fortress, 1985).

[2] Arthur Kleinman, *Patients and Healers in the Context of Culture: An Exploration of the Borderland between Anthropology, Medicine, and Psychiatry* (Berkeley: University of California Press, 1980), 24. The concept of a health care system is also emphasized by other anthropologists, see George M. Foster, "Disease Etiologies in Non-Western Medical Systems," *American Anthropologist* 78 (1976): 773–82; George M. Foster and B. G. Anderson, *Medical Anthropology* (New York: John Wiley & Sons, 1978); Thomas M. Johnson and Carolyn E. Sargent, *Medical Anthropology* (New York: Praeger, 1990).

[3] There have been other rubrics applied to the study of systems of healing, medicine, etc. The rubric "health care system" is preferable to "healing system" because the latter restricts its focus to healing instead of including the maintenance of health and the prevention of illness. The frequent associations of the rubric "medical system" with modern medicine may be misleading in the study of the ancient world.

[4] Of course, studying ancient cultures involves translating their cultural and religious categories into modern ones. Terms such as *patient, contagion,* and *illness* do not always have exact equivalents in ancient cultures. Nonetheless, we generally will use the term *illness* to speak of any physical or behavioral condition that was considered abnormal in a person by an ancient culture. We use the term *disease* to identify a condition that has a modern medical equivalent (e.g., "malaria"). We use the term *patient* to identify anyone thought to have an illness in any culture. Likewise the term *contagion* refers to the idea that an illness could spread (e.g., the condition usually translated as "leprosy" in English), even when such an idea was not based on modern germ theory.

[5] Kleinman, *Patients and Healers;* Arthur Kleinman and B. Good, eds., *Culture and Depression* (Berkeley: University of California Press, 1985).

[6] Mirko D. Grmek, *Diseases in the Ancient Greek World* (Baltimore: Johns Hopkins University Press, 1989).

[7] Vivian Nutton's important works include "Social History of Graeco-Roman Medicine," in *Medicine in Society* (ed. A. Wear; Cambridge: Cambridge University Press, 1992), 15–58; and "Roman Medicine, 250 BC to AD

200," in *The Western Medical Tradition, 800 BC to AD 1800* (ed. Conrad et al.), 39–70.

[8] Henry E. Sigerist, *A History of Medicine* (2 vols.; New York: Oxford University Press, 1951–1961).

[9] See esp. McNeill, *Plagues and Peoples*.

[10] *LABS* 296, rev., lines 3–14; Parpola does not document his diagnosis of the Akkadian phrase GIG diᶜu as malaria. My explanation of the deities are in parenthesis, and the words in brackets are based on reconstructions by Parpola.

[11] Ibid., 255, lines 8–13.

[12] My translation. "Leprosy" may describe a variety of skin diseases here.

[13] Foster, "Disease Etiologies," 773–82

[14] Pilch, "Sickness and Healing in Luke–Acts," 201.

[15] Mary Douglas's theory is primarily outlined in *Purity and Danger: An Analysis of Concepts of Purity and Taboo* (London: Routledge & Kegan Paul, 1966). Florence R. Kluckhohn and Fred L. Strodtbeck, *Variations in Value Orientation* (New York: Harper & Row, 1961).

[16] Other recent discussions of the concept of purity include Hannah K. Harrington, *The Impurity Systems of Qumran and the Rabbis: Biblical Foundations* (Atlanta: Scholars Press, 1993); Howard Eilberg-Schwartz, *The Savage in Judaism: An Anthropology of Israelite Religion and Ancient Judaism* (Bloomington: Indiana University Press, 1990).

[17] Pilch, "Sickness and Healing in Luke–Acts," 183.

[18] Ibid., 184.

[19] Ibid., 186, 208, 209.

[20] All English translations of 4QMMT are those of Qimron and Strugnell. They use brackets to signify reconstructed portions of the text, and parentheses to clarify their translations.

[21] Qimron and Strugnell, *Miqṣat Maᶜaśe Ha-Torah,* 161.

[22] On the relationship between health and stages of civilization, see Mark Nathan Cohen, *Health and the Rise of Civilization* (New Haven: Yale University Press, 1989).

[23] Plato, *Republic* 3.407E (Shorey, LCL): ἀλλὰ τὸν μὴ δυνάμενον ἐν τῇ καθεστηκυίᾳ περιόδῳ ζῆν μὴ οἴεσθαι δεῖν θεραπεύειν, ὡς οὔτε αὑτῷ οὔτε πόλει λυσιτελῆ.

[24] Ibid., 3.406D: Τέκτων μέν . . . κάμνων ἀξιοῖ παρὰ τοῦ ἰατροῦ φάρμακον. . . . . ἐὰν δέ τις αὐτῷ μακρὰν δίαιταν προστάττῃ, πιλίδιά τε περὶ τὴν κεφαλὴν περιτιθεὶς καὶ τὰ τούτοις ἑπόμενα, ταχὺ εἶπεν ὅτι οὐ σχολὴ κάμνειν οὐδὲ λυσιτελεῖ οὕτω ζῆν, νοσήματι τὸν νοῦν προσέχοντα, τῆς δὲ προκειμένης ἐργασίας ἀμελοῦντα.

[25] Susan Treggiari, "Domestic Staff at Rome during the Julio-Claudian Period, 27 B.C. to A.D. 68," *Histoire sociale/Social History* 6 (1973): 241–55.

[26] A more detailed summary of these typologies is found in Avalos, *Illness and Health Care in the Ancient Near East.*

²⁷For the impact of economics on health care options, see William C. Cockerham, *Medical Sociology* (6th ed.; Englewood Cliffs, N.J.: Prentice Hall, 1995), 118–32.

²⁸Linda M. Hunt, "Inequalities in the Mexican Health Care System: Problems in Managing Cancer in Southern Mexico," in *Society, Health, and Disease: Transcultural Perspectives* (ed. Janardan Subedi and Eugene B. Gallagher; Upper Saddle River, N.J.: Prentice-Hall, 1996), 139.

²⁹See further Winifred S. Blackman, *The Fallāhin of Upper Egypt* (London: George G. Harrap, 1927), 187; Geraldine Pinch, *Magic in Ancient Egypt* (Austin: University of Texas Press, 1994), 60, 104–19.

NOTES TO CHAPTER 2 (pages 33–45)

¹For a detailed discussion of the evolution of the Israelite health care systems, see Avalos, *Illness and Health Care in the Ancient Near East.*

²11QTemple 45:12–13: ולוא יטמאו את העיר; following the editio princeps of Yigael Yadin, מגלת המקדש (2 vols; Jerusalem: The Israel Exploration Society and the Shrine of the Book, 1977), 2:136. See also 2 Sam 5:8.

³See similar comments by Eilberg-Schwartz, *The Savage in Judaism,* 183. For a cross-cultural study of menstrual customs, see T. Buckley and Alma Gottlieb, *Blood Magic: The Anthropology of Menstruation* (Berkeley: University of California Press, 1988).

⁴Plato, *Republic* 3.408B (Shorey, LCL): νοσώδη δὲ φύσει τε καὶ ἀκόλαστον οὔτε αὐτοῖς οὔτε τοῖς ἄλλοις ᾤοντο λυσιτελεῖν ζῆν, οὐδ' ἐπὶ τούτοις τὴν τέχνην δεῖν εἶναι, οὐδὲ θεραπευτέον αὐτούς, οὐδ' εἰ Μίδου πλουσιώτεροι εἶεν.

⁵See also D. J. Wiseman, "A New Text of the Babylonian Poem of the Righteous Sufferer," *AnSt* 30 (1980): 101–7.

⁶See Richardson, *Herod,* 76–77; see also Bert Edwards Park, *The Impact of Illness on World Leaders* (Philadelphia: University of Pennsylvania Press, 1986).

⁷K. Y. Mumcuoglu and J. Zias, "How the Ancients Deloused Themselves," *BAR* 15 (6, 1989): 66–68.

⁸For a brief general study, see N. L. Etkin, "Ethnopharmacology: Biology and Behavioral Perspectives in the Study of Indigenous Medicines," in Johnson and Sargent, *Medical Anthropology,* 149–58.

⁹L. E. Stager, "Why Were Hundreds of Dogs Buried at Ashkelon?" *BAR* 17 (3, 1991): 27–42. For other sites with dog burials in Israel, including a recent find at the Ben Gurion Airport, see Paula Wapnish and Brian Hesse, "Pampered Pooches or Plain Pariahs? The Ashkelon Dog Burials," *BA* 56 (2, 1993): 55–80.

¹⁰For a recent discussion of pharmaceuticals in the biblical period, see Walter Jacob, "Medicinal Plants in the Bible," in *The Healing Past: Pharma-*

ceuticals in the Biblical and Rabbinic World (ed. Irene Jacob and Walter Jacob; Leiden: E. J. Brill, 1993), 27–46.

[11] [Hershel Shanks], "The Balm of Gilead," *BAR* 22 (5, 1996): 18–19, 24.

[12] Joseph Zias and K. Numeroff, "Ancient Dentistry in the Eastern Mediterranean: A Brief Overview," *IEJ* 36 (1986): 65–67.

[13] See comments by W. G. Dever, "Material Remains and the Cult in Ancient Israel: An Essay in Archaeological Systematics," in *The Word of the Lord Shall Go Forth: Essays in Honor of David Noel Freedman in Celebration of His Sixtieth Birthday* (ed. Carol L. Meyers and M. O'Connor; Winona Lake, Ind.: Eisenbrauns, 1983), 578–79.

[14] See T. A. Holland, "A Study of Palestinian Iron Age Baked Clay Figurines, with Special Reference to Jerusalem: Cave 1," *Levant* 9 (1977): 121–55; and Abdel-Jalil 'Amr, "Ten Human Clay Figurines from Jerusalem," *Levant* 20 (1988): 185–96.

[15] Carol Meyers, *Discovering Eve: Ancient Israelite Women in Context* (New York: Oxford University Press, 1988), 161–63.

[16] The Aramaic text of the *Targum Onqelos* is that in A. M. Silbermann, ed., *Chumash with Rashi's Commentary* (5 vols.; Jerusalem: Silbermann, 1934), 2:112.

[17] Bronze serpents have been found in temples (e.g., the Asclepieion at Pergamum) known to have been used for therapy during the first millennium B.C.E. Bronze serpents, such as those found in or near shrines at Timna, Tell Mevorakh, and Hazor from the Late Bronze Age, may have been used in therapeutic rituals, but other functions cannot be excluded.

[18] See *DSST* 127.

[19] We ought not assume, however, that all mention of abnormal blood flow referred to the reproductive organs as the source. See further Amy-Jill Levine, "Discharging Responsibility: Matthean Jesus, Biblical Law, and Hemorrhaging Woman," in *Treasures New and Old: Recent Contributions to Matthean Studies* (ed. David R. Bauer and Mark Allan Powell; Atlanta: Scholars Press, 1996), 379–97.

NOTES TO CHAPTER 3 (pages 49–58)

[1] Edelstein and Edelstein, *Asclepius,* 2:1–10.

[2] Ibid., 2:91–101.

[3] Strabo, *Geographica* 9.5.17 = T. 714.

[4] Edelstein and Edelstein, *Asclepius,* 2:248.

[5] For a recent study of materials relating to Asclepius at Epidauros, see Lynn R. LiDonnici, The *Epidaurian Miracle Inscriptions: Text, Introduction, and Commentary* (Texts and Translations 36; Graeco-Roman Religion Series 11; Atlanta:Scholars, 1995).

[6] See Susan M. Sherwin-White, *Ancient Cos: A Historical Study from the Dorian Settlement to the Imperial Period* (Göttingen: Vandenhoeck & Ruprecht, 1978).

[7] See Wolfgang Radt, *Pergamon: Geschichte und Bauten, Funde und Erforschung einer antiken Metropole* (Cologne: Du Mont, 1988).

[8] See Sara B. Aleshire, *The Athenian Asklepieion: The People, Their Dedications, and the Inventories* (Amsterdam: J. C. Gieben, 1989).

[9] See Carl Roebuck, *Corinth XIV: The Asklepieion and Lerna* (Princeton: American School of Classical Studies at Athens, 1951); R. Struckmann, *Important Medical Centers in Antiquity: Epidaurus and Corinth* (Athens: Editions Kansas, 1979). According to Roebuck (p. 154), the cult was introduced in the late fifth century B.C.E., and it rose to a grand scale, even if only locally, in the late fourth century B.C.E.

[10] Edelstein and Edelstein, *Asclepius*, 2:249.

[11] See Filippo Coarelli, ed., *Fregellae 2. Il santuario di Esculapio* (Rome: Tognon, 1986).

[12] Maria Aurenhammer, "Sculptures of Gods and Heroes from Ephesos," in *Ephesos: Metropolis of Asia* (ed. Koester), 266–67.

[13] See J. L. Angel, "The Bases of Paleodemography," *American Journal of Physical Anthropology* 30 (1969): 427–38; idem, "Ecology and Population in the Eastern Mediterranean," *World Archaeology* 4 (1972): 88–105.

[14] B. E. Richardson, *Old Age among the Ancient Greeks* (Baltimore: Johns Hopkins University Press, 1933).

[15] Grmek, *Diseases*, 104.

[16] For a study of the effects of the food supply on the health of ancient Greece, see Robert Sallares, *The Ecology of the Ancient Greek World* (Ithaca: Cornell University Press, 1991).

[17] The plague is described by Thucydides, 2.47–55. Modern studies include those of J. F. D. Shrewsbury, "The Plague of Athens," *Bulletin of the History of Medicine* 24 (1950): 1–25; and J. N. Longrigg, "The Great Plague of Athens," *History of Science* 18 (1980): 209–25.

[18] Edelstein and Edelstein, *Asclepius*, 1:431.

[19] Alexander Fuks, *Social Conflict in Ancient Greece* (Leiden: E. J. Brill, 1984), 14. See also G. E. M. de Ste. Croix, *The Class Struggle in the Ancient Greek World* (Ithaca: Cornell University Press, 1981).

[20] Andrew Lintott, *Violence, Civil Strife, and Revolution in the Classical City* (London: Croom Helm, 1982). See also E. Ruschenbusch, *Untersuchungen zu Staat und Politik in Griechenland vom 7.–4. Jr. v. Chr.* (Bamberg: Aku, 1978).

[21] Lintott, *Violence, Civil Strife, and Revolution*, 251–62.

[22] On the use of Asclepieia as refuges, see Nanno Marinatos and Robin Hagg, *Greek Sanctuaries: New Approaches* (New York: Routledge, 1995).

[23] Witt, *Isis*, 185. This discussion of Isis is also indebted to Sarolta A. Takács, *Isis and Sarapis in the Roman World* (Leiden: E. J. Brill, 1995).

[24] Witt, *Isis*, 186.

[25] Kee, *Medicine*, 91.

[26] See J. Gwyn Griffiths, *The Origin of Osiris and His Cult* (Leiden: E. J. Brill, 1980).

[27] Frayne, E.4.1.7.2001, line 3: *nin lú-ku₅-da(?) dím-dí[m]*. The transliteration and translation follow corrections to the Sumerian text made by P. Steinkeller (personal communication).

[28] Ibid., E.4.2.13.22, line 12.

[29] See Jan Bergman, *Ich bin Isis: Studien zum memphitischen Hintergrund der griechischen Isisaretalogien* (Uppsala: Uppsala Academy, 1968); Dieter Müller, *Ägypten und die griechischen Isis-Aretalogien* (Berlin: Akademie, 1961); R. Harder, *Karpokrates von Chalkis und die memphitische Isis-Propaganda* (Berlin: de Gruyter, 1943). On the influence of Isis aretalogies on Jewish literature, see John S. Kloppenborg, "Isis and Sophia in the Book of Wisdom," *HTR* 75 (1, 1982): 57–84. For a hymn to Gula, see W. G. Lambert, "The Gula Hymn of Bulluṭsa-rabi," *Or* 36 (1967): 105–33.

[30] V. F. Vanderlip, ed., *The Four Greek Hymns of Isidorus* (Toronto: Haklert, 1972), 2, 7–8.

[31] Witt, *Isis*, 258.

[32] Juvenal, *Satires* 13 (Ramsay, LCL): "decernat quodcumque volet de corpore nostro Isis et irato feriat mea lumina sistro."

[33] Translation follows N. E. Scott, "The Metternich Stela," *Bulletin of the Metropolitan Museum of Art* 9 (1951): 201–17; A. Klasens, *A Magical Statue Base (Socle behague) in the Museum of Antiquities at Leiden* (Leiden: Brill, 1952); and John F. Nunn, *Ancient Egyptian Medicine* (London: British Museum, 1996), 109–10.

[34] Plutarch, *Isis and Osiris* 63.

[35] Witt, *Isis*, 61.

[36] Ibid., 53.

[37] Robert Turcan, *The Cults of the Roman Empire* (trans. Antonia Nevill; London: Blackwell, 1996), 77.

[38] Ibid., 90.

[39] Albert Henrichs, "Vespasian's Visit to Alexandria," *ZPE* 3 (1968): 51–56

[40] Turcan, *Cults*, 76.

[41] See Amos Kloner, "Underground Metropolis: The Subterranean World of Maresha," *BAR* 23 (2, 1997): 35.

[42] Frederick Norris, "Isis, Serapis, and Demeter in Antioch of Syria," *HTR* 75 (2, 1982), 189–207.

[43] Turcan, *Cults*, 95.

[44] Ernest Renan, *Marc-Aurèle et la fin du monde antique* (Paris: Calmann-Lévy, 1923), 579: "si le christianisme eût été arreté dans sa croissance par quelque maladie mortelle, le monde eût été mithraiste."

[45] See Per Beskow, "Tertullian on Mithras," in *Studies in Mithraism* (ed. John R. Hinnells; Rome: Bretschneider, 1994), 51–60.

[46] Plutarch, *Life of Pompey* 24, 7. See also A. L. Frothingham, "The Cosmopolitan Religion of Tarsus and the Origin of Mithra," *AJA* 22 (1918): 63–64.

⁴⁷For general studies of Mithraism, see Hinnells, *Studies in Mithraism;* Turcan, *Cults,* 195–247; and David Ulansey, *The Origins of the Mithraic Mysteries: Cosmology As Salvation in the Ancient World* (New York: Oxford University Press, 1988).

⁴⁸Ulansey, *Mithraic Mysteries,* 6.

⁴⁹Lewis Hopfe, "Archaeological Indications on the Origins of Roman Mithraism," in *Uncovering Ancient Stones: Essays in Memory of H. Neil Richardson* (ed. L. M. Hopfe; Winona Lake, Ind.: Eisenbrauns, 1994), 147–56.

⁵⁰Ibid., 155.

⁵¹Franz Cumont collected a mass of materials about Mithras in his celebrated *Textes et monuments figurés relatifs aux mystères de Mithra* (2 vols.; Brussels: Lamertin, 1896–1899).

⁵²E.g., Philip G. Kreyenbroek, "Mithra and Ahriman in Iranian Cosmogonies," in *Studies in Mithraism* (ed. Hinnells), 173–82.

⁵³Beskow, "Tertullian on Mithras," 51–60.

⁵⁴Turcan, *Cults,* 209.

⁵⁵This discussion of secular Greco-Roman traditions is here indebted to Vivian Nutton, "Medicine in the Greek World, 800–50 BC," in *The Western Medical Tradition, 800 BC to AD 1800* (ed. Conrad et al.), 11–38; and "Roman Medicine, 250 BC to AD 200."

⁵⁶See J. Longrigg, *Greek Rational Medicine* (London: Routledge, 1993).

⁵⁷Celsus, *De medicina,* Proemium, 9–10.

⁵⁸See Wesley D. Smith, *The Hippocratic Tradition* (Ithaca: Cornell University Press, 1979).

⁵⁹Hippocrates, *Sacred Disease* 5.15–6.24 (Jones, LCL). ἕτερον δὲ μέγα τεκμήριον ὅτι οὐδέν θειότερόν ἐστι τῶν λοιπῶν νοσημάτων. Τοῖσι γὰρ φλεγματώδεσι φύσει γίνεται. Τοῖσι δέ χολώδεσιν οὐ προσπίπτει ... Ἀλλὰ γὰρ αἴτιος ὁ ἐγκέφαλος τούτου τοῦ πάθεος, ὥσπερ καὶ τῶν ἄλλων νοσημάτων τῶν μεγίστων.

⁶⁰On the history of the classification of epilepsy, see Owsei Temkin, *The Falling Sickness: A History of Epilepsy from the Greeks to the Beginnings of Modern Neurology* (Baltimore: Johns Hopkins University Press, 1971).

⁶¹See, e.g., Wesley D. Smith, "Notes on Ancient Medical Historiography," *Bulletin of the History of Medicine* 63 (1989): 73–109.

⁶²See Nutton, "Social History of Graeco-Roman Medicine," 24.

⁶³Sigerist, *A History of Medicine,* 2:333.

⁶⁴Nutton, "Roman Medicine, 250 BC to AD 200," 66–67.

⁶⁵R. Walzer, *Galen on Jews and Christians* (London: Oxford University Press, 1949).

⁶⁶Ibid., 15.

NOTES TO CHAPTER 4 (pages 61–71)

¹See Douglas R. Edwards, *Religion and Power: Pagans, Jews, and Christians in the Greek East* (New York: Oxford University Press, 1996), 62.

[2] Hayman, "Monotheism—a Misused Word?" 1–15.

[3] Douglas L. Penney and Michael O. Wise, "By the Power of Beelzebub: An Aramaic Incantation Formula from Qumran (4Q560)," *JBL* 113 (4, 1994): 627.

[4] Ibid., 632.

[5] Accordingly, I agree with the position of Twelftree (*Jesus the Exorcist*, 49–51) against Wesley Carr (*Angels and Principalities* [Cambridge: Cambridge University Press, 1981]), who argues that the concept of mighty forces from which man sought relief was not prevalent in the first century.

[6] Aelian, *Nature of Animals* 11:33 = T. 422.

[7] See further G. W. Allen, *The Death of Herod: The Narrative and Theological Function of Retribution in Luke–Acts* (Atlanta: Scholars Press, 1997).

[8] Hermann Binder, "Die angebliche Krankheit des Paulus," *TZ* 32 (1, 1976): 1–13.

[9] E.g., Robert M. Price, "Illness Theodicies in the New Testament," *Journal of Religion and Health* 25 (4, 1986): 310.

[10] Klaus Seybold and Ulrich B. Mueller, *Sickness and Healing* (trans. D. W. Stott; Nashville: Abingdon, 1978), 168; Mueller is responsible for the section on the New Testament.

[11] Hippocrates, *Nature of Man* 4 (Jones, LCL): Τὸ δὲ σῶμα τοῦ ἀνθρώπου ἔχει ἐν ἑωυτῷ αἷμα καὶ φλέγμα καὶ χολὴν ξανθήν καὶ μέλαιναν καὶ ταῦτ' ἐστὶν αὐτῷ ἡ φύσις τοῦ σώματος, καὶ διὰ ταῦτα ἀλγεῖ καὶ ὑγιαίνει.

[12] Such scholars include Marcus Borg, *Meeting Jesus Again for the First Time* (San Francisco: HarperCollins, 1994); and N. T. Wright, *The New Testament and the People of God* (Minneapolis: Fortress, 1992).

[13] Paula Fredriksen, "Did Jesus Oppose the Purity Laws?" *BRev* (June 1995): 23.

[14] The Hebrew word for lepers here is צרועים; appearing elsewhere in the *Temple Scroll* is מצורעם. See further Qimron and Strugnell, *Miqsat Ma'ase Ha-Torah*, 138.

[15] See also Lawrence Schiffman, "Purity and Perfection: Exclusion from the Council of the Community in the Serekh Ha-Edah," in *Biblical Archaeology Today: Proceedings of the International Congress on Biblical Archaeology, Jerusalem, April 1984* (ed. Janet Amitai; Jerusalem: Israel Exploration Society, 1985), 373–89.

[16] Josephus, *Against Apion* 1.282–283. For a general discussion of medicine in the works of Josephus, see Samuel S. Kottek, *Medicine and Hygiene in the Works of Flavius Josephus* (Leiden: E. J. Brill, 1994).

[17] Josephus, *Against Apion*, 1.281 (Thackeray, LCL): τοῖς γὰρ λεπρῶσιν ἀπείρηκε μήτε μένειν ἐν πόλει μήτ' ἐν κώμῃ κατοικεῖν, ἀλλὰ μόνους περιπατεῖν κατεσχισμένους τὰ ἱμάτια, καὶ τὸν ἀψάμενον· αὐτῶν ἢ ὁμωρόφιον γενόμενον οὐ καθαρὸν ἡγεῖται.

[18] Ibid., 1.284: οὐ μόνον δὲ περὶ τῶν λεπρῶν οὕτως ἐνομοθέτησεν.

[19] For a discussion whether Luke 17:11–19 is Lukan or pre-Lukan, see Joseph A. Fitzmyer, *The Gospel according to Luke: Introduction, Translation, and Notes* (2 vols.; AB 28–28A; Garden City, N.Y.: Doubleday, 1981–1985), 2:1149–52.

[20] See Christopher J. Cowton, "The Alms Trade: A Note on Identifying the Beautiful Gate of Acts 3.2," *NTS* 42 (1996): 475–76.

[21] Suetonius, *Claudius* 25.2: "Cum quidam et adfecta mancipia in insulam Aesculapi taedio medendi exponerent, omnes qui exponerentur liberos esse sanxit." My translation.

[22] Josephus, *Against Apion* 1.288–292.

[23] Ibid., 1.295–311.

[24] Porphyry, *De abstinentia* 2.19 = T. 318: ἐν γοῦν Ἐπιδαύρῳ προεγέγραπτο. ἁγνὸν χρὴ ναοῖο θυώδεος ἐντὸς ἰόντα ἔμμεναι· ἁγνεία δ' ἐστὶ φρονεῖν ὅσια.

[25] Aelius Aristides, *Oratio* 39.1–18 = T. 804: μόνον δὲ τοῦτο τὸ αὐτὸ νοσοῦσι καὶ ὑγιαίνουσιν ὁμοίως, ἥδιστον καὶ λυσιτελέστατον ἑκατέροις τε καὶ συναμφοτέροις ἐστίν. . . . τὸ δὲ τῷ σῴζειν τοὺς χρωμένους, οὐ τῷ μηδένα αὐτοῦ ψαύειν, ἱερόν ἐστιν· καὶ τὸ αὐτὸ καθαρσίοις τε ἐξαρκεῖ τοῖς περὶ τὸ ἱερὸν καὶ ἀνθρώποις καὶ πίνειν καὶ λούεσθαι καὶ προσορῶσιν εὐφραίνεσθαι.

[26] C. S. Mann, *Mark: A New Translation with an Introduction and Commentary* (AB 27; New York: Doubleday, 1986), 315, suggests that such a statement was so dissimilar to what was found in Judaism that it may well reach back to an authentic tradition about Jesus.

[27] See further Jerome H. Neyrey, "The Idea of Purity in Mark's Gospel," *Semeia* 35 (1996): 91–128.

[28] For a critique of scholars who have interpreted Matthean redaction of healing stories in Mark as a sign of disinterest in healing, see John Paul Heil, "Significant Aspects of the Healing Miracles in Matthew," *CBQ* 41 (1, 1979): 274–87. Another scholar who sees Matthew as interested in healing throughout his Gospel is Joseph A. Comber, "The Verb *Therapeuō* in Matthew's Gospel," *JBL* 97 (3, 1978): 431–34.

[29] For similar interpretations of Christianity's purity laws, see John L. White, "Jesus as Actant," *BR* 26 (1991): 19–29.

NOTES TO CHAPTER 5 (pages 75–87)

[1] *t. Ḥul.* 22.23; cited in E. E. Urbach, *The Sages: Their Concepts and Beliefs* (2 vols.; Jerusalem: Magnes, 1975), 1:116.

[2] Naveh and Shaked, *Magic Spells and Formulae*, 123 (Bowl 18:5–6).

[3] Following Émile Puech, "11QPsAp^a : Un rituel d'exorcismes: Essai de reconstruction," *RevQ* 14 (3, 1990): 377–408.

[4] Ibid., 387.

[5] *y. Ber.* 9.12 p. 13a; cited in Urbach, *The Sages*, 1:182.

[6] *PGM* CXVII (Betz). See also Antonio Carlini et al., eds., *Papiri letterari greci* (Pisa: Giardini, 1978), no. 34.

[7] See Stambaugh, *The Ancient Roman City,* 135.

[8] Celsus, *De medicina* 6.6.8b (Jones, LCL): "At si neque medicus neque medicamentum praesto est, sepius utrumlibet horum in oculus penicillo ad id ipsum facto infusum id malum lenit."

[9] See Treggiari, "Domestic Staff."

[10] Ibid., 254.

[11] See H. Eschebach, "Die Artzhäuser in Pompeji," *Antike Welt* 15 (Sondernummer, 1984), 1–79; Georg Harig, "Zum Problem 'Krankenhaus' in der Antike," *Klio* 53 (1971): 179–95.

[12] מִתְרַפְּאִין מֵהֶם רְפוּי מָמוֹן אֲבָל לֹא רְפוּי נְפָשׁוֹת, following J. Armitage Robinson, *The Mishna on Idolatry: 'Aboda Zara* (TS 8; 1911; repr., Nendeln: Kraus, 1967), 29–30.

[13] Sijbolt Noorda, "Illness and Sin, Forgiving and Healing: The Connection of Medical Treatment and Religious Beliefs in Sira 38, 1–15," in *Studies in Hellenistic Religions* (ed. J. Vermaseren; Leiden: E. J. Brill, 1979), 215–24.

[14] Josephus, *Life* 403–404.

[15] R. Kudlien, "Jüdische Ärzte im römischen Reich," *Medizinhistorisches Journal* 20 (1985): 36–57.

[16] Celsus, *De medicina* 5.22.4; see further Kudlien, "Jüdische Ärzte," 48.

[17] See Malka Hershkovitz, "A Roman Cupping Vessel from the Masada Excavations," in *Judea and the Greco-Roman World in the Time of Herod in the Light of Archaeological Evidence* (ed. Klaus Fittschen and Gideon Foerster; Göttingen: Vandenhoeck & Ruprecht, 1996), 171–73.

[18] Zias and Numeroff, "Ancient Dentistry."

[19] Seneca, *On Benefits* 6.15.2: "Emis a medico rem inestimabilem, vitam ac bonam valetudinem."

[20] Pliny the Elder, *Natural History* 29.5.11 (Jones, LCL): "hinc illae circa aegros miserae sententiarum concertationes, nullo idem censente, ne videatur accessio alterius. hinc illa infelix monumentis inscriptio, turba se medicorum perisse."

[21] Galen, *On Physicians* 45.

[22] Ibid., 47.

[23] Dioscorides, *De materia medica,* Book 5 (Max Wellman, ed.; Berlin: Weidmann, 1914); John Riddle, *Dioscorides on Pharmacy and Medicine* (Austin: University of Texas Press, 1985).

[24] For Rufus, see Manfred Ulmann, *Rufus von Ephesos: Krankenjournale* (Wiesbaden: Otto Harrasowitz, 1978).

[25] On the date of the Wisdom of Solomon in the first century and, more specifically, during the reign of Caligula, see David Winston, *The Wisdom of Solomon* (AB 43; New York: Doubleday, 1979), 20–25.

[26] Josephus, *Jewish War* 2.136.

[27] Richardson, *Herod,* 203; H. M. Cotton and J. Geiger, *Masada II: Latin and Greek Documents* (Jerusalem: The Israel Exploration Society, 1989), 133.

[28] Celsus, *De medicina* 2.33.6 (Spencer, LCL): "His autem omnibus, et simplicibus et permixtis, varie medici utuntur, ut magis quid quisque persuaserit sibi appareat, quam quid evidenter compererit."

[29] Apuleius, *Metamorphoses* 5.10 (Hanson, LCL): "Ego vero maritum articulari etiam morbo complicatum curvatumque ac per hoc rarissimo Venerem meam recolentem sustineo, plerumque detortos et duratos in lapidem digitos eius perfricans, fomentis olidis et pannis sordidis et foetidis cataplasmatibus manus tam delicatas istas adurens, nec uxoris officiosam faciem, sed medicae laboriosam personam sustinens."

[30] Joseph Zias, "Death and Disease in Ancient Israel," *BA* 54 (3, 1991): 146–59.

[31] Celsus, *De medicina* 8.2.3–6.

[32] Ibid., 7.7.1.

[33] Ibid., 10.1 (Spencer, LCL): "Sanguinem incisa vena mitti novum non est: sed nullum paene esse morbum, in quo non mittatur novum est."

[34] Ibid., 3.21.2 (Spencer, LCL): "Facilius in servis quam in liberis tollitur, quia, cum desideret, famem, sitim, mille alia taedia longamque patientiam, promptius iis succurritur, qui facile coguntur, quam quibus inutilis libertas est."

[35] Ignatius, *To the Ephesians* 7.2 (Lake, LCL): εἷς ἰατρός ἐστιν, σαρκικός τε καὶ πνευματικός . . . Ἰησοῦς Χριστὸς ὁ κύριος ἡμῶν.

[36] Meier (*A Marginal Jew,* 2:543) notes, e.g., that Luke tends more than Mark to see faith as a result produced by miracles. See also Christopher D. Marshall, *Faith As a Theme in Mark's Narrative* (Cambridge: Cambridge University Press, 1989).

[37] E. N. Jackson, *The Role of Faith in the Process of Healing* (London: SCM, 1981).

[38] Tatian, *Oratio ad Graecos* 18: φαρμακεία δὲ καὶ πᾶν τὸ ἐν αὐτῇ εἶδος τῆς αὐτῆς ἐστιν ἐπιτεχνήσεως. εἰ γάρ τις ὑπὸ τῆς ὕλης θεραπεύεται πιστεύων αὐτῇ, θεραπευθήσεται μᾶλλον αὐτὸς δυνάμει θεοῦ προσανέχων. ὥσπερ γὰρ τὰ δηλητήρια συνθέσεις εἰσὶν ὑλικαί, τὸν αὐτὸν τρόπον καὶ τὰ ἰώμενα τῆς αὐτῆς ὑποστάσεως ἐστιν.

[39] Nutton, "Medicine in Late Antiquity and the Early Middle Ages," 74.

[40] Crossan, *The Historical Jesus,* 344.

[41] Justin, *Second Apology* 6 (*ANF* 1:190).

[42] Tertullian, *To Scapula* 4.

[43] See Bruce M. Metzger, *The Text of the New Testament: Its Transmission, Corruption, and Restoration* (3d ed.; New York: Oxford University Press, 1992), 226–29.

[44] Bruce M. Metzger, *A Textual Commentary on the Greek New Testament* (London: United Bible Societies, 1975), 101.

[45] See J. F. Wimmer, *Fasting in the New Testament* (New York: Paulist, 1982).

[46] Origen, *Against Celsus* 1.6 (*ANF* 4:399).

[47] For discussions of the issues surrounding magic, including the history of its definitions, see David Aune, "Magic in Early Christianity," *ANRW* 23.2:1507–57; Fritz Graf, *Magic in the Ancient World* (trans. Franklin Philip; Cambridge: Harvard University Press, 1997); John M. Hull, *Hellenistic Magic and the Synoptic Tradition* (London: SCM, 1974); Georg Luck, *Arcana Mundi: Magic and the Occult in the Greek and Roman Worlds* (Baltimore: Johns Hopkins University Press, 1985), 3–60; Remus, *Pagan-Christian Conflict over Miracle*.

[48] For other critiques of Kee's distinctions, see Crossan, *The Historical Jesus*, 306.

[49] Kee, *Medicine*, 3.

[50] Ibid., 124.

[51] *AMT* 9.1:27–28: *liddi*(SUB-*di*) ^{d}*Gu-la tê*(TU$_6$) *balāṭi*(TI.LA) *en-qu-ti ṣim-de-ti li-qer-ri-bu at-ti taš-ku-ni ba-laṭ bu-ul-ṭi*. The text and translation follow Benno Landsberger, "Corrections to the Article: 'An Old Babylonian Charm against Merḫu,'" *JNES* 17 (1958): 56.

[52] Crossan, *The Historical Jesus*, 305.

[53] Susan Garrett, *The Demise of the Devil*, 4–5.

NOTES TO CHAPTER 6 (pages 91–95)

[1] Jackson, *Doctors and Diseases*, 56.

[2] Louis Cohn-Haft, "The Public Physicians of Ancient Greece," *Smith College Studies in History* 42 (1956): 44.

[3] Turcan, *Cults*, 111.

[4] Pliny the Elder, *Natural History* 29.1: "cum sit fructuosior nulla."

[5] Ibid., 29.2 (Jones, LCL): "Nec fuit postea quaestus modus, quoniam Prodicus Selymbriae natus, e discipulis eius, instituit quam vocant iatrilipticen et unctoribus quoque medicorum ac mediastinis vectigal invenit."

[6] Galen, *On Physicians* 45.

[7] Nutton, "Social History of Graeco-Roman Medicine," 40.

[8] T. 464b. See comments in Timothy S. Miller, *The Birth of the Hospital in the Byzantine Empire* (Baltimore: Johns Hopkins University Press, 1985), 40.

[9] Aelian, *Fragments* 101 = T. 455.

[10] For examples, see Aleshire, *The Athenian Asklepieion*. For a discussion of expensive votive offerings from a non-Asclepian healing shrine in the first century B.C.E., see T. W. Potter, "A Republican Healing Sanctuary at Ponte di Nona Near Rome and the Classical Tradition of Votive Medicine," *Journal of the British Archaeological Association* 138 (1985): 23–47.

[11] Libanius, *Declamationes* 34.23–26 = T. 539.

[12] Apuleius, *Metamorphoses* 11.30 (Hanson, LCL): "omnibus ex studio pietatis magis quam mensura rerum mearum collatis."

¹³ Ibid., 11.28 (Hanson, LCL): "Nam et viriculas patrimonii pere-
grinationis attriverant impensae, et erogationes urbicae pristinis illis pro-
vincialibus antistabant plurimum."
¹⁴ Engels, Roman Corinth, 57, 101.
¹⁵ Plutarch, Isis and Osiris 80.
¹⁶ Philostratus, Life of Apollonius of Tyana 7.39 (Conybeare, LCL):
ἀρώματά τε ὁπόσα ἡ Ἰνδικὴ κηπεύει, καὶ χρήματα μὲν αὐτοὺς λαμπρὰ
ὑπὲρ τούτων πράττονται, ξυνδρῶσι δὲ οὐδέν.
¹⁷ See examples in Christopher A. Faraone and Dirk Obbink, Magika
Hiera: Ancient Greek Magic and Religion (New York: Oxford University Press,
1991), 110–15. See further Vivian Nutton, "From Medical Certainty to Medical Amulets: Three Aspects of Ancient Therapeutics," Clio Medica 22 (1991):
13–22.
¹⁸ Metzger (Textual Commentary, 145) and Fitzmyer (Luke, 2:746)
regard the clause ἰατροῖς προσαναλώσασα ὅλον τὸν βίον as most
questionable.
¹⁹ Tertullian, Apology 14.5 (Glover and Rendall, LCL): "avaritae mer-
ito, quia medicinam nocenter exercerbat."
²⁰ Didache 11.12 (Lake, LCL): δός μοι ἀργύρια ἢ ἕτερά τινα. For a recent discussion of the Didache, see C. N. Jefford, ed., The Didache in Context:
Essays on Its Text, History, and Transmission (NovTSup 77; Sheffield: Sheffield Academic, 1995). On the seeming inconsistency in the Didache's attitude toward the remuneration of prophets, see Stephen J. Patterson,
"Didache 11–13: The Legacy of Radical Itinerancy in Early Christianity,"
ibid., 313–27.
²¹ Irenaeus, Against Heresies 22.4 (ANF 1:409).
²² Tertullian, Apology 39.5 (Glover and Rendall, LCL): "Etiam si
quod arcae genus est, non de honoraria summa quasi redemptae religionis
congregatur."

NOTES TO CHAPTER 7 (pages 99–107)

¹ Ramsay MacMullen, Christianizing the Roman Empire, A.D. 100–400
(New Haven: Yale University Press, 1984), 41.
² See Jackson, Doctors and Diseases, 65–66.
³ Eschebach, "Die Arzthäuser in Pompeji," 8.
⁴ J. Donald Hughes, Pan's Travail: Environmental Problems in the Ancient Greeks and the Romans (Baltimore: Johns Hopkins University Press,
1994), 160.
⁵ Pliny the Elder, Natural History 31.8.11 (Jones, LCL): "vitiligines
tolli."
⁶ Ibid., 31.8.12.
⁷ Josephus, Jewish Antiquities 17.169–176.

[8] See Ronny Reich, "The Hot Bath-House *(balneum)*, the *Miqweh*, and the Jewish Community in the Second Temple Period," *JJS* 39 (1, 1988): 102–7.

[9] See Yizhar Hirschfeld and Giora Siolar, "The Roman Thermae at Hammat Gader: Preliminary Reports of Three Seasons of Excavation," *IEJ* 31 (1981), 197–219.

[10] Edelstein and Edelstein, *Asclepius*, 2:191.

[11] Pausanius, *Descriptio Graeciae* 10.32.12 = T. 499.

[12] Ibid., 8.54.5 = T. 772.

[13] T. 834: ὀφρὺς ἱκανῶς ὀρθία.

[14] Themistius, *Oratio* 27 = T. 385: εἰ τὰ σώματα ἐνοσοῦμεν καὶ ἐδεόμεθα τῆς παρὰ τοῦ Θεοῦ βοηθείας, ὁ δὲ ἐνταῦθα παρῆν ἐν τῷ νεῷ καὶ τῇ ἀκροπόλει καὶ παρεῖχεν ἑαυτὸν τοῖς κάμνουσιν, ὥσπερ δήποτε καὶ λέγεται, πότερον ἦν ἀναγκαῖον εἰς Τρίκκην Βαδίζειν καὶ διαπλεῖν εἰς Ἐπίδαυρον κατὰ τὸ παλαιὸν κλέος, ἢ δύο Βήματα κινηθέντας ἀπηλλάχθαι τοῦ νοσήματος.

[15] Apuleius, *Metamophoses* 11.19.

[16] Turcan, *Cults*, 109. See also R. A. Wild, "The Known Isis-Serapis Sanctuaries from the Roman Period," *ANRW* 17.4:1739–1851; M. Malaise, *Inventaire préliminaire des documents égyptiens découverts en Italie* (EPRO 21; Leiden: E. J. Brill, 1972), 289ff.

[17] See further Malaise, *Inventaire préliminaire*, 187–215.

[18] See E. J. Hobsbawm, *Bandits* (New York: Penguin, 1985); and Richard Horsely and J. Hanson, *Bandits, Prophets, and Messiahs* (Minneapolis: Winston, 1985).

[19] Richardson, *Herod*, 250–52.

[20] Libanius, *Oratio* 30.39 = T. 817: Καὶ νῦν οὓς ἄγει μὲν εἰς Κιλικίαν νοσήματα, τῆς τοῦ Ἀσκληπιοῦ χρήζοντα χειρός αἱ δὲ περὶ τὸν τόπον ὕβρεις ἀπράκτους ἀποπέμπουσι.

[21] Cited in Witt, *Isis*, 191.

[22] Strabo, *Geographica* 8.6.15 = T. 735: τὸ ἱερὸν πλῆρες ἔχοντος ἀεὶ τῶν τε καμνόντων.

[23] Galen, *On Physicians* 93.

[24] See Nutton, "The Patient's Choice," 248.

[25] Galen, *On Physicians* 113.

[26] Crossan, *The Historical Jesus*, 332–33.

[27] It is not within the scope of this study to show that the Cynics, who were characterized by a wandering lifestyle, influenced Christianity, but it does not seem that healing was a part of Cynic itinerancy. For recent discussions of the question of Cynic influence, see F. Gerald Downing, "Deeper Reflections on the Jewish Cynic Jesus," *JBL* 117 (1, 1998): 97–104; Paul Rhodes Eddy, "Jesus As Diogenes? Reflections on the Cynic Jesus Thesis," *JBL* 115 (3, 1996): 449–69; and David Seeley, "Jesus and the Cynics Revisited," *JBL* 116 (4, 1997): 704–12.

²⁸ Franz Annen, *Heil für Heiden: Zur Bedeutung und Geschichte der Tradition vom besessenen Gerasener (Mk, 5, 1–20 parr.)* (Frankfurt: Josef Knecht, 1976), 199: "Jesus hat sicher als Exorzist gewirkt, mit grosser Wahrscheinlichkeit auch ausserhalb des jüdischen Gebietes und an Heiden."

²⁹ See Frost, *Christian Healing,* 109.

³⁰ See Walzer, *Galen on Jews and Christians,* 38

³¹ See Frost, *Christian Healing,* 109.

³² *Didache* 11.6 (Lake, LCL): ἐὰν δὲ ἀργύριον αἰτῇ ψευδοπροφήτης ἐστι.

NOTES TO CHAPTER 8 (pages 111–114)

¹ See *DSST,* 42.

² Schiffman, *Reclaiming the Dead Sea Scrolls,* 280.

³ Ibid., 281.

⁴ For a recent review of the evidence concerning observance of the Sabbath in the first century, see Yang Yong-Eui, *Jesus and the Sabbath in Matthew's Gospel* (Sheffield: Sheffield Academic, 1997).

⁵ Galen, *On Physicians* 89.

⁶ T. 421:641–643: ἀρ' ἀγγέλλεται χρηστόν τι; τοῦτο γὰρ ποθοῦσ' ἐγὼ πάλαι ἔνδον κάθημαι περιμένουσα τουτονί.

⁷ On the problems and methodology of demography in the study of Roman civilization, see Tim G. Parkin, *Demography and Roman Society* (Baltimore: Johns Hopkins University Press, 1992).

⁸ Shaw, "Seasons of Death," 117.

⁹ Ibid., 120.

¹⁰ Cohn-Haft, "The Public Physician," 31. In contrast, Libanius (*Declamationes* 34.38–42 = T. 540) complains of being cramped by innumerable physicians (πόθεν οὖν τῷ πλήθει τῶν ἰατρῶν στενοχωρούμεθα;) in the fourth century C.E.

NOTES TO CHAPTER 9 (pages 117–119)

¹ On these developments, see Amundsen, *Medicine,* 175–247; and Kelsey, *Healing and Christianity,* 125–85.

Bibliography

Aleshire, Sara B. *The Athenian Asklepieion: The People, Their Dedications, and the Inventories.* Amsterdam: J. C. Gieben, 1989.

Allen, G. W. *The Death of Herod: The Narrative and Theological Function of Retribution in Luke–Acts.* Atlanta: Scholars Press, 1997.

'Amr, Abdel-Jalil. "Ten Human Clay Figurines from Jerusalem." *Levant* 20 (1988): 185–96.

Amundsen, Darrel W. *Medicine, Society, and Faith in the Ancient Medieval Worlds.* Baltimore: Johns Hopkins University Press, 1996.

Angel, J. L. "The Bases of Paleodemography." *American Journal of Physical Anthropology* 30 (1969): 427–38.

_____. "Ecology and Population in the Eastern Mediterranean." *World Archaeology* 4 (1972): 88–105.

The Ante-Nicene Fathers. Ed. Alexander Roberts and James Donaldson. 1885–1887. Repr., 10 vols. Peabody: Hendrickson, 1994.

Annen, Franz. *Heil für Heiden: Zur Bedeutung und Geschichte der Tradition vom besessenen Gerasener (Mk, 5, 1–20 parr.).* Frankfurt: Josef Knecht, 1976.

Apostolic Fathers. Trans. Kirsopp Lake. 2 vols. LCL. Cambridge: Harvard University Press, 1913.

Apuleius. Trans. J. Arthur Hanson. 2 vols. LCL. Cambridge: Harvard University Press, 1989.

Aune, David. "Magic in Early Christianity." *ANRW* 23.2:1507–57. Part 2, *Principat,* 23.2. Ed. H. Temporini and W. Haase. New York: de Gruyter, 1980.

Aurenhammer, Maria. "Sculptures of Gods and Heroes from Ephesos." Pages 251–80 in *Ephesos: Metropolis of Asia*. Ed. Helmut Koester. Valley Forge, Penn.: Trinity Press International, 1995.

Avalos, Hector. *Illness and Health Care in the Ancient Near East: The Role of the Temple in Greece, Mesopotamia, and Israel*. Harvard Semitic Monographs 54. Atlanta: Scholars Press, 1995.

_____. "Medicine." Pages 450–59 in vol. 3 of *The Oxford Encyclopedia of Archaeology in the Near East*. Ed. E. M. Meyers. 5 vols. New York: Oxford University Press, 1997.

Baumgarten, Joseph M. "The 'Halakah' in *Miqṣat Maʿase ha-Torah* (MMT)." *Journal of the American Oriental Society* 116 (3, 1996): 512–16.

Bellizoni, Arthur J. Jr., ed. *The Two Source Hypothesis: A Critical Appraisal*. Macon, Ga.: Mercer, 1985.

Bergman, Jan. *Ich bin Isis: Studien zum memphitischen Hintergrund der griechischen Isisaretalogien*. Uppsala: Uppsala Academy, 1968.

Bernstein, Moshe J., ed. *Reading 4QMMT: New Perspectives on Qumran Law and History*. Atlanta: Scholars Press, 1996.

Beskow, Per. "Tertullian on Mithras." Pages 51–60 in *Studies in Mithraism*. Ed. John R. Hinnells. Rome: Bretschneider, 1994.

Betz, H. D., ed. *The Greek Magical Papyri in Translation, Including the Demotic Spells*. 2d ed. Chicago: University of Chicago Press, 1996.

Binder, Hermann. "Die angebliche Krankheit des Paulus." *Theologische Zeitschrift* 32 (1, 1976): 1–13.

Black, F. L. "Measles Endemicity in Insular Populations: Critical Community Size and Its Evolutionary Implications." *Journal of Theoretical Biology* 11 (1966): 207–11.

Blackman, Winifrid S. *The Fallāhin of Upper Egypt*. London: George G. Harrap, 1927.

Bokser, Baruch M. "Recent Developments in the Study of Judaism, 70–200 C.E." *Second Century* 3 (1983): 1–68.

Borg, Marcus. *Meeting Jesus Again for the First Time*. San Francisco: HarperCollins, 1994.

Buckley, Thomas, and Alma Gottlieb, eds. *Blood Magic: The Anthropology of Menstruation*. Berkeley: University of California Press, 1988.

Carlini, Antonio, et al., eds. *Papiri letterari greci*. Pisa: Giardini, 1978.

Carr, Wesley. *Angels and Principalities*. Cambridge: Cambridge University Press, 1981.

Celsus. *De medicina*. Trans. W. G. Spencer. 3 vols. LCL. Cambridge: Harvard University Press, 1935–1938.

Charlesworth, James H. *Jesus and the Dead Sea Scrolls: The Controversy Resolved.* New York: Doubleday, 1992.

Coarelli, Filippo, ed. *Fregellae 2. Il santuario di Esculapio.* Rome: Tognon, 1986.

Cockburn, T. Aidan. "Infectious Diseases in Ancient Populations." *Current Anthropology* 12 (1971): 51–56.

Cockerham, William C. *Medical Sociology.* 6th ed.. Englewood Cliffs, N.J.: Prentice Hall, 1995.

Cohen, Mark N. *Health and the Rise of Civilization.* New Haven: Yale University Press, 1989.

Cohn-Haft, Louis. "The Public Physicians of Ancient Greece." *Smith College Studies in History* 42 (1956): 1–91.

Comber, Joseph A. "The Verb *Therapeuō* in Matthew's Gospel." *Journal of Biblical Literature* 97 (3, 1978): 431–34.

Cotton, H. M., and J. Geiger. *Masada II: Latin and Greek Documents.* Jerusalem: The Israel Exploration Society, 1988.

Cowton, Christopher J. "The Alms Trade: A Note on Identifying the Beautiful Gate of Acts 3.2." *New Testament Studies* 42 (1996): 475–76.

Croix, G. E. M. de Ste. *The Class Struggle in the Ancient Greek World.* Ithaca: Cornell University Press, 1981.

Cross, F. M., and Esther Eshel. "The Missing Link." *Biblical Archeology Review* (1998): 48–53, 69.

———. "Ostraca from Khirbet Qumran." *Israel Exploration Journal* 47 (1997): 17–28.

Crossan, J. D. *The Birth of Christianity: Discovering What Happened in the Years Immediately after the Execution of Jesus.* San Francisco: HarperSanFrancisco, 1998.

———. *The Historical Jesus: The Life of a Jewish Mediterranean Peasant.* New York: Harper & Row, 1991.

———. "Open Healing and Open Eating: Jesus as Jewish Cynic?" *Biblical Research* 36 (1991): 6–18.

Cumont, Franz. *Textes et monuments figurés relatifs aux mystères de Mithra.* 2 vols. Brussels: Lamertin, 1896–1899.

Davies, Stevan L. *Jesus the Healer: Possession Trance and the Origins of Christianity.* New York: Continuum, 1995.

Dever, W. G. "Material Remains and the Cult in Ancient Israel: An Essay in Archaeological Systematics." Pages 571–87 in *The Word of the Lord Shall Go Forth: Essays in Honor of David Noel Freedman in Celebration of His Sixtieth Birthday.* Ed. Carol L. Meyers and M. O'Connor. Winona Lake, Ind.: Eisenbrauns, 1983.

Didache. The Apostolic Fathers. Vol. 1. Ed. Kirsopp Lake. 2 vols. LCL. Cambridge: Harvard University Press, 1913.

Dioscuridis. De materia medica, Book 5. Max Wellmann, ed. Berlin: Weidmann, 1914.

Douglas, Mary. *Purity and Danger: An Analysis of Concepts of Purity and Taboo.* London: Routledge & Kegan Paul, 1966.

Downing, F. Gerald. "Deeper Reflections on the Jewish Cynic Jesus." *Journal of Biblical Literature* 117 (1, 1998): 97–104.

Eddy, Paul Rhodes. "Jesus as Diogenes? Reflections on the Cynic Jesus Thesis." *Journal of Biblical Literature* 115 (3, 1996): 449–69.

Edelstein, Ludwig, and Emma Edelstein. *Asclepius.* 2 vols. Baltimore: Johns Hopkins University Press, 1945.

Edwards, Douglas R. *Religion and Power: Pagans, Jews, and Christians in the Greek East.* New York: Oxford University Press, 1996.

Edwards, Douglas R., and C. Thomas McCollough, eds. *Archaeology and the Galilee: Texts and Contexts in the Graeco-Roman and Byzantine Periods.* Atlanta: Scholars Press, 1997.

Eilberg-Schwartz, Howard. *The Savage in Judaism: An Anthropology of Israelite Religion and Ancient Judaism.* Bloomington: Indiana University Press, 1990.

Engels, Donald. *Roman Corinth.* Chicago: University of Chicago Press, 1990.

Epp, Eldon J., and George W. MacRae, eds. *The New Testament and Its Modern Interpreters.* Philadelphia: Fortress, 1989.

Eschebach, Hans. "Die Arzthäuser in Pompeji." *Antike Welt* 15 (Sondernummer, 1984): 1–79.

Etkin, N. L. "Ethnopharmacology: Biology and Behavioral Perspectives in the Study of Indigenous Medicines." Pages 149–58 in *Medical Anthropology.* Ed. T. M. Johnson and C. E. Sargent. New York: Praeger, 1990.

Faraone, Christopher A., and Dirk Obbink. *Magika Hiera: Ancient Greek Magic and Religion.* New York: Oxford University Press, 1991.

Farmer, William R. *New Synoptic Studies.* Macon, Ga.: Mercer, 1983.

Ferngren, Gary B. "Early Christianity as a Religion of Healing." *Bulletin of the History of Medicine* 66 (1992): 1–15.

Fitzmyer, Joseph. *The Gospel according to Luke: Introduction, Translation, and Notes.* 2 vols. AB 28–28A. Garden City, N.Y.: Doubleday, 1981–1985.

Fontaine, Carole. "Disabilities and Illness in the Bible: A Feminist Perspective," Pages 286–300 in *A Feminist Companion to the*

Hebrew Bible and the New Testament. Ed. Athalya Brenner; Sheffield: Sheffield Academic Press, 1996.

Foster, George M. "Disease Etiologies in Non-Western Medical Systems." *American Anthropologist* 78 (1976): 773–82.

Foster, George M., and B.G. Anderson. *Medical Anthropology.* New York: John Wiley & Sons, 1978.

Foucault, Michel. *The Birth of the Clinic.* New York: Vintage, 1973.

Fredriksen, Paula. "Did Jesus Oppose the Purity Laws?" *Bible Review* (June 1995) 18–25, 42–46.

Frost, Evelyn. *Christian Healing: A Consideration of the Place of Spiritual Healing in the Church of Today in the Light of the Ante-Nicene Church.* London: A. R. Mowbray & Co., 1949.

Frothingham, A. L. "The Cosmopolitan Religion of Tarsus and the Origin of Mithra." *American Journal of Archaeology* 22 (1918): 63–64.

Fuks, Alexander. *Social Conflict in Ancient Greece.* Leiden: E. J. Brill, 1984.

Galen, *De optimo medico cognoscendo libelli versionem arabicam primum edidit, in linguam anglicam vertit, commentatus est Albert Z. Iskander.* Edited by Albert Z. Iskander. Corpus medicorum graecorum supplementum orientale 4. Berlin: Akademie, 1988.

Garrett, Susan R. *The Demise of the Devil: Magic and the Demonic in Luke's Writings.* Minneapolis: Fortress, 1989.

Gesler, William M. *The Cultural Geography of Health Care.* Pittsburgh: University of Pittsburgh Press, 1991.

Golb, Norman. *Who Wrote the Dead Sea Scrolls? The Search for the Secret of Qumran.* New York: Scribner, 1996.

Grabbe, Lester L. *Judaism from Cyrus to Hadrian.* 2 vols. Minneapolis: Fortress, 1992.

Graf, Fritz. *Magic in the Ancient World.* Trans. Franklin Philip. Cambridge: Harvard University Press, 1997.

Griffiths, J. Gwyn. *The Origin of Osiris and His Cult.* Leiden: E. J. Brill, 1980.

Grmek, Mirko D. *Diseases in the Ancient Greek World.* Baltimore: Johns Hopkins University Press, 1989.

Harder, R. *Karpokrates von Chalkis und die memphitische Isis-Propaganda.* Berlin: de Gruyter, 1943.

Harig, Georg. "Zum Problem 'Krankenhaus' in der Antike." *Klio* 53 (1971): 179–95.

Harnack, Adolf von. "Medicinisches aus der ältesten Kirchengeschichte." *Texte und Untersuchungen zur Geschichte der altchristlichen Literatur* (TUGAL) 8 (4, 1892): 37–152.

Harrington, Hannah K. *The Impurity Systems of Qumran and the Rabbis: Biblical Foundations*. Atlanta: Scholars Press, 1993.

Hayman, Peter. "Monotheism—a Misused Word in Jewish Studies?" *Journal of Jewish Studies* 42 (1, 1991): 1–15.

Heil, John Paul. "Significant Aspects of the Healing Miracles in Matthew." *Catholic Biblical Quarterly* 41 (1, 1979): 274–87.

Henrichs, Albert. "Vespasian's Visit to Alexandria." *Zeitschrift für Papyrologie und Epigraphik* 3 (1968): 51–60.

Hershkovitz, Malka. "A Roman Cupping Vessel from the Masada Excavations." Pages 171–73 in *Judea and the Greco-Roman World in the Time of Herod in the Light of Archaeological Evidence*. Ed. Klaus Fittschen and Gideon Foerster. Göttingen: Vandenhoeck & Ruprecht, 1996.

Hinnells, John R., ed. *Studies in Mithraism*. Rome: Bretschneider, 1994.

Hippocrates. Trans. W. H. S. Jones. 4 vols. LCL. Cambridge: Harvard University Press, 1923–1931.

Hirschfeld, Yizhar, and Giora Siolar. "The Roman Thermae at Hammat Gader: Preliminary Reports of Three Seasons of Excavation." *Israel Exploration Journal* 31 (1981): 197–219.

Hobsbawm, E. J. *Bandits*. New York: Penguin, 1985.

Holland, T. A. "A Study of Palestinian Iron Age Baked Clay Figurines, with Special Reference to Jerusalem: Cave 1." *Levant* 9 (1977): 121–55.

Homer. *The Iliad*. Trans. A. T. Murray. 2 vols. LCL. Cambridge: Harvard University Press, 1924–1925.

Hopfe, Lewis. "Archaeological Indications on the Origins of Roman Mithraism." Pages 137–56 in *Uncovering Ancient Stones: Essays in Memory of H. Neil Richardson*. Ed. L. M. Hopfe. Winona Lake, Ind.: Eisenbrauns, 1994.

Horsely, Richard, and J. Hanson. *Bandits, Prophets, and Messiahs*. Minneapolis: Winston, 1985.

Hughes, J. Donald. *Pan's Travail: Environmental Problems in the Ancient Greeks and the Romans*. Baltimore: Johns Hopkins University Press, 1994.

Hull, John M. *Hellenistic Magic and the Synoptic Tradition*. London: SCM, 1974.

Humphrey, Peggy. *María Atkinson—la Madre de Mexico: No Doubt Here*. Cleveland, Tenn.: Pathway, 1967.

Hunt, Linda M. "Inequalities in the Mexican Health Care System: Problems in Managing Cancer in Southern Mexico." Pages 130–40 in *Society, Health, and Disease: Transcultural Perspec-*

_____. "The Great Plague of Athens." *History of Science* 18 (1980): 209–25.

Lovering, Eugene H., ed. *1993 SBL Seminar Papers*. Atlanta: Scholars Press, 1993.

Luck, Georg. *Arcana Mundi: Magic and the Occult in the Greek and Roman Worlds*. Baltimore: Johns Hopkins University Press, 1985.

Lührmann, Dieter. "Neutestamentliche Wundergeschichten und antike Medizin." Pages 195–204 in *Religious Propaganda and Missionary Competition in the New Testament World*. Ed. Lukas Borman, Kelly Del Tredici, and Angela Standharatinger. Leiden: E. J. Brill, 1994.

MacMullen, Ramsay. *Christianizing the Roman Empire, A.D. 100–400*. New Haven: Yale University Press, 1984.

Majno, Guido. *The Healing Hand*. Cambridge: Harvard University Press, 1975.

Malaise, Michel. *Inventaire préliminaire des documents égyptiens découverts en Italie*. Études preliminaires aux religions orientales dans l'empire romain 21. Leiden: E. J. Brill, 1972.

Malina. Bruce J. *Christian Origins and Cultural Anthropology*. Atlanta: John Knox, 1986.

Mann, Christopher Stephen. *Mark: A New Translation with an Introduction and Commentary*. AB 27. New York: Doubleday, 1986.

Marinatos, Nanno, and Robin Hagg. *Greek Sanctuaries: New Approaches*. New York: Routledge, 1995.

Marshall, Christopher D. *Faith As a Theme in Mark's Narrative*. Cambridge: Cambridge University Press, 1989.

Martinez, Florentino García. *The Dead Sea Scrolls Translated: The Qumran Texts in English*. Leiden: E. J. Brill, 1994.

Mason, Steve. "The Study of Early Judaism: A Dialogue with Lester Grabbe." *Journal of the American Oriental Society* 118 (3, 1995): 463–72.

McNeill, William H. *Plagues and Peoples*. New York: Doubleday, 1976.

McNicol, Allan J., ed. *Beyond the Q Impasse—Luke's Use of Matthew*. Valley Forge, Penn.: Trinity Press International, 1996.

Meier, John P. *A Marginal Jew: Rethinking the Historical Jesus*. 2 vols. New York: Doubleday, 1991–1994.

Metzger, Bruce M. *The Text of the New Testament: Its Transmission, Corruption, and Restoration*. 3d ed. New York: Oxford University Press, 1992.

_____. *A Textual Commentary on the Greek New Testament*. London: United Bible Societies, 1975.

Meyers, Carol. *Discovering Eve: Ancient Israelite Women in Context*. New York: Oxford University Press, 1988.

Meyers, Eric M. "Jesus in his Galilean Context." Pages 57–66 in *Archaeology and the Galilee: Texts and Contexts in the Graeco-Roman and Byzantine Periods*. Ed. Douglas R. Edwards and C. Thomas McCollough. Atlanta: Scholars Press, 1997.

_____, ed. *Oxford Encyclopedia of Archaeology in the Near East*. 5 vols. New York: Oxford University Press, 1997.

Millar, Fergus. *The Roman Near East, 31 BC–AD 337*. Cambridge: Harvard University Press, 1993.

Miller, Timothy S. *The Birth of the Hospital in the Byzantine Empire*. Baltimore: Johns Hopkins University Press, 1985.

Moore, George F. *Judaism in the First Centuries of the Christian Era: The Age of the Tannaim*. 1927. Repr., Peabody, Mass.: Hendrickson, 1997.

Morris, Brian. *Anthropological Studies of Religion: An Introductory Text*. Cambridge: Cambridge University Press, 1987.

Müller, Dieter. *Ägypten und die griechischen Isis-Aretalogien*. Berlin: Akademie, 1961.

Mumcuoglu, K. Y., and J. Zias. "How the Ancients Deloused Themselves." *Biblical Archeology Review* 15 (6, 1989): 66–68.

Naveh, Joseph, and Shaul Shaked. *Magic Spells and Formulae: Aramaic Incantations of Late Antiquity*. Jerusalem: Magnes, 1993.

Neusner, Jacob. *Rabbinic Literature and the New Testament: What We Cannot Show, We Do Not Know*. Valley Forge, Penn.: Trinity Press International, 1994.

Neyrey, Jerome H. "The Idea of Purity in Mark's Gospel." *Semeia* 36 (1986): 91–128.

Noorda, Sijbolt. "Illness and Sin, Forgiving and Healing: The Connection of Medical Treatment and Religious Beliefs in Sira 38, 1–15." Pages 215–24 in *Studies in Hellenistic Religions*. Ed. J. Vermaseren. Leiden: E. J. Brill, 1979.

Norris, Frederick. "Isis, Serapis, and Demeter in Antioch of Syria." *Harvard Theological Review* 75 (2, 1982): 189–207.

Nunn, John F. *Ancient Egyptian Medicine*. London: British Museum, 1996.

Nutton, Vivian. "From Medical Certainty to Medical Amulets: Three Aspects of Ancient Therapeutics." *Clio Medica* 22 (1991): 13–22.

_____. "Healers in the Medical Market Place: Towards a Social History of Graeco-Roman Medicine." Pages 15–58 in *Medicine in*

Society. Ed. Andrew Wear. Cambridge: Cambridge University Press, 1992.

_____. "Medicine in the Greek World, 800–50 BC." Pages 11–38 in *The Western Medical Tradition, 800 BC to AD 1800*. Ed. Lawrence Conrad et al. Cambridge: Cambridge University Press, 1995.

_____. "Medicine in Late Antiquity and the Early Middle Ages." Pages 71–91 in *The Western Medical Tradition, 800 BC to AD 1800*. Ed. Lawrence Conrad et al. Cambridge: Cambridge University Press, 1995.

_____. "Murders and Miracles: Lay Attitudes toward Medicine in Classical Antiquity." Pages 23–53 in *Patients and Practitioners: Lay Perceptions of Medicine in Pre-industrial Society*. Ed. Roy Porter. Cambridge: Cambridge University Press, 1985.

_____. "The Patient's Choice: A New Treatise by Galen." *Classical Quarterly* 40 (1, 1990): 236–57.

_____. "Roman Medicine, 250 BC to AD 200." Pages 39–70 in *The Western Medical Tradition, 800 BC to AD 1800*. Ed. Lawrence Conrad et al. Cambridge: Cambridge University Press, 1995.

Park, Bert Edwards. *The Impact of Illness on World Leaders*. Philadelphia: University of Pennsylvania Press, 1986.

Parkin, Tim G. *Demography and Roman Society*. Baltimore: Johns Hopkins University Press, 1992.

Parpola, Simo, ed. *Letters from Assyrian and Babylonian Scholars*. State Archives of Assyria 10. Helsinki: Helskinki University Press, 1993.

Patterson, Stephen J. "Didache 11–13: The Legacy of Early Itinerancy in Early Christianity." Pages 313–27 in *The Didache in Context: Essays in Its Text, History, and Transmission*. Ed. Clayton N. Jefford. Leiden: E. J. Brill, 1995.

Pausanias. Trans. W. H. S. Jones, H. A. Omerod, and R. E. Wycherley. 5 vols. LCL. Cambridge: Harvard University Press, 1918–1935.

Penney, Douglas L., and Michael O. Wise. "By the Power of Beelzebub: An Aramaic Incantation Formula from Qumran (4Q560)." *Journal of Biblical Literature* 113 (4, 1994): 627.

Philostratus. Trans. F. C. Conybeare. 2 vols. LCL. Cambridge, Mass.: Harvard University Press, 1912.

Pilch, J. J. "Biblical Leprosy and Body Symbolism." *Biblical Theology Bulletin* 11 (4, 1981): 108–13.

_____. "Healing in Mark: A Social Science Analysis." *Biblical Theology Bulletin* 15 (4, 1985): 142–50.

_____. "The Health Care System in Matthew: A Social Science Analysis." *Biblical Theology Bulletin* 16 (3, 1986): 281–83.

_____. "Sickness and Healing in Luke–Acts." Pages 181–209 in *The Social World of Luke–Acts*. Ed. Jerome Neyrey. Peabody, Mass.: Hendrickson, 1991

Pinch, Geraldine. *Magic in Ancient Egypt*. Austin: University of Texas Press, 1994.

Plato. *Republic*. Trans. Paul Shorey et al. 2 vols. LCL. Cambridge: Harvard University Press, 1930–1935.

Pliny. *Natural History*. Trans. D. E. Eichholz, W. H. S. Jones, and H. Rackham. 10 vols. LCL. Cambridge: Harvard University Press, 1938–1963.

Plutarch. Trans. Frank Cole Babbit et al. 26 vols. LCL. Cambridge: Harvard University Press, 1936–1961.

Potter, T. W. "A Republican Healing Sanctuary at Ponte di Nona near Rome and the Classical Tradition of Votive Medicine." *Journal of the British Archaeological Association* 138 (1985): 23–47.

Price, Robert M. "Illness Theodicies in the New Testament." *Journal of Religion and Health* 25 (4, 1986): 309–15.

Puech, Émile. "11QPsApᵃ: Un rituel d'exorcismes: Essai de reconstruction." *Revue de Qumran* 14 (3, 1990): 377–408.

Qimron, Elisha, and John Strugnell, eds. *Qumran Cave 4*. Vol. 5. *Miqṣat Maʿaśe Ha-Torah*. Discoveries in the Judaean Desert 10. Oxford: Clarendon, 1994.

Radt, Wolfgang. *Pergamon: Geschichte und Bauten, Funde und Erforschung einer antiken Metropole*. Cologne: Du Mont, 1988.

Reich, Ronny. "The Hot Bath-House (*balneum*), the *Miqweh*, and the Jewish Community in the Second Temple Period." *Journal of Jewish Studies* 39 (1, 1988): 102–7.

Remus, Harold. *Jesus As Healer*. Cambridge: Cambridge University Press, 1997.

_____, *Pagan-Christian Conflict over Miracle in the Second Century*. Cambridge, Mass.: Philadelphia Patristic Foundation, 1983.

Renan, Ernest. *Marc-Aurèle et la fin du monde antique*. Paris: Calmann-Lévy, 1923.

Richardson, B. E. *Old Age among the Ancient Greeks*. Baltimore: Johns Hopkins University Press, 1933.

Richardson, Peter. *Herod: King of the Jews and Friend of the Romans*. Columbia: University of South Carolina Press, 1996.

Riddle, John. *Dioscorides on Pharmacy and Medicine*. Austin: University of Texas Press, 1985.

Robinson, J. Armitage. *The Mishna on Idolatry: 'Aboda Zara.* Texts and Studies 8. 1911. Repr., Nendeln: Kraus, 1967.

Roebuck, Carl. *Corinth XIV: The Asklepieion and Lerna.* Princeton: American School of Classical Studies at Athens, 1951.

Rotberg, Robert I., and Theodore K. Rabb, eds. *Hunger and History: The Impact of Changing Food Production and Consumption Patterns of Society.* Cambridge: Cambridge University Press, 1985.

Roth, S. J. *The Blind, the Lame, and the Poor: Character Types in Luke–Acts.* Sheffield: Sheffield Academic, 1997.

Ruschenbusch, E. *Untersuchungen zu Staat und Politik in Griechenland vom 7.–4. Jr. v. Chr.* Bamberg: Aku, 1978.

Saldarini, Anthony J. *Pharisees, Scribes, and Sadducees in Palestinian Society.* Wilmington, Del.: Glazier, 1988.

Sallares, Robert. *The Ecology of the Ancient Greek World.* Ithaca: Cornell University Press, 1991.

Schiffman, Lawrence. "Purity and Perfection: Exclusion from the Council of the Community in the Serekh Ha-Edah." Pages 373–89 in *Biblical Archaeology Today: Proceedings of the International Congress on Biblical Archaeology, Jerusalem, April 1984.* Ed. Janet Amitai. Jerusalem: Israel Exploration Society, 1985.

_____. *Reclaiming the Dead Sea Scrolls.* New York: Doubleday, 1994.

Schwartz, Daniel R. "MMT, Josephus, and the Pharisees." Pages 67–80 in *Reading 4QMMT: New Perspectives on Qumran Law and History.* Ed. John Kampen and Moshe J. Bernstein. Atlanta: Scholars Press, 1996.

Scott, N. E. "The Metternich Stela." *Bulletin of the Metropolitan Museum of Art* 9 (1951): 201–17.

Seeley, David. "Jesus and the Cynics Revisited." *Journal of Biblical Literature* 116 (4, 1997): 704–12.

Seneca. *Moral Essays: De beneficiis.* Trans. John W. Basore. LCL. Cambridge: Harvard Univeristy Press, 1935.

Seybold, Klaus, and Ulrich B. Mueller. *Sickness and Healing.* Trans. D. W. Stott. Nashville: Abingdon, 1978.

[Shanks, Hershel.] "The Balm of Gilead." *Biblical Archeology Review* 22 (5, 1996): 18–19, 24.

Shaw, Brent D. "Seasons of Death: Aspects of Mortality in Imperial Rome." *Journal of Roman Studies* 86 (1996): 100–138.

Sherwin-White, Susan. M. *Ancient Cos: A Historical Study from the Dorian Settlement to the Imperial Period.* Göttingen: Vandenhoeck & Ruprecht, 1978.

Shrewsbury, J. F. D. "The Plague of Athens." *Bulletin of the History of Medicine* 24 (1950): 1–25.

Sigerist, Henry E. *A History of Medicine*. 2 vols. New York: Oxford University Press, 1951–1961.

Silbermann, A. M., ed. *Chumash with Rashi's Commentary*. 5 vols. Jerusalem: Silbermann, 1934.

Smith, Morton. *Jesus the Magician*. San Francisco: Harper & Collins, 1978.

Smith, Wesley D. *The Hippocratic Tradition*. Ithaca: Cornell University Press, 1979.

————. "Notes on Ancient Medical Historiography." *Bulletin of the History of Medicine* 63 (1989): 73–109.

Stager, L. E. "Why Were Hundreds of Dogs Buried at Ashkelon?" *Biblical Archeology Review* 17 (3, 1991): 27–42.

Stambaugh, John E. *The Ancient Roman City*. Baltimore: Johns Hopkins University Press, 1988.

Stark, Rodney. *The Rise of Christianity: A Sociologist Reconsiders History*. Princeton: Princeton University Press, 1996.

Stemberger, Günter. *Jewish Contemporaries of Jesus: Pharisees, Sadducees, Essenes*. Minneapolis: Fortress, 1995.

Struckmann, R. *Important Medical Centers in Antiquity: Epidaurus and Corinth*. Athens: Editions Kansas, 1979.

Suetonius. Trans. J. C. Rolfe. 2 vols. LCL. Cambridge: Harvard University Press, 1914.

Takács, Sarolta A. *Isis and Sarapis in the Roman World*. Leiden: E. J. Brill, 1995.

Tatian. *Oratio ad Graecos and Fragments*. Ed. Molly Whittaker. Oxford: Clarendon, 1982.

Temkin, Owsei. *The Falling Sickness: A History of Epilepsy from the Greeks to the Beginnings of Modern Neurology*. Baltimore: Johns Hopkins University Press, 1971.

Tertullian. *Apology/De Spectaculis*. Trans. T. R. Glover and G. H. Rendall. LCL. Cambridge: Harvard University Press, 1931.

————. *To Scapula*. Trans. Rudolph Arbesman. *Tertullian: Apologetical Works and Minucius Felix Octavius*. New York: Fathers of the Church, 1950.

Theissen, Gerd. *Sociology of Early Palestinian Christianity*. Trans. John Bowden. Philadelphia: Fortress, 1978.

Theissen, Gerd, and Annette Merz. *The Historical Jesus: A Comprehensive Guide*. Trans. John Bowden. Minneapolis: Fortress, 1998.

Thomas, John Christopher. *The Devil, Disease, and Deliverance: Origins of Illness in New Testament Thought*. Sheffield: Sheffield Academic Press, 1998.

Thucydides. Trans. Charles Foster Smith. 4 vols. LCL. Cambridge Harvard University Press, 1919–1923.

Treggiari, Susan. "Domestic Staff at Rome in the Julio-Claudian Period, 27 B.C. to A.D. 68." *Histoire sociale/Social History* 6 (1973): 241–55.

Trunk, Dieter. *Der messianische Heiler: Eine redaktions- und religionsgeschichtliche Studie zu den Exorzismen im Matthäusevangelium.* Freiberg: Herder, 1994.

Turcan, Robert. *The Cults of the Roman Empire.* Trans. Antonia Nevill. London: Blackwell, 1996.

Twelftree, Graham H. *Jesus the Exorcist: A Contribution to the Study of the Historical Jesus.* Peabody, Mass.: Hendrickson, 1993.

Ulansey, David. *The Origins of the Mithraic Mysteries: Cosmology as Salvation in the Ancient World.* New York: Oxford University Press, 1988.

Ulmann, Manfred, *Rufus von Ephesos: Krankenjournale.* Wiesbaden: Otto Harrasowitz, 1978.

Urbach, E. E. *The Sages: Their Concepts and Beliefs.* 2 vols. Jerusalem: Magnes, 1975.

Vanderlip, V. F., ed. *The Four Greek Hymns of Isidorus.* Toronto: Haklert, 1972.

Vermes, Geza. *Jesus the Jew: A Historian's Reading of the Gospels.* Philadelphia: Fortress, 1981.

———. "Methodology in the Study of Jewish Literature in the Graeco-Roman Period." *Journal of Jewish Studies* 36 (2, 1985): 145–57.

Walzer, R. *Galen on Jews and Christians.* London: Oxford University Press, 1949.

Wapnish, Paula, and Brian Hesse. "Pampered Pooches or Plain Pariahs? The Ashkelon Dog Burials." *Biblical Archaeologist* 56 (2, 1993): 55–80.

Wells, Colin. *The Roman Empire.* 2d ed. Cambridge: Harvard University Press, 1992.

White, John L. "Jesus as Actant." *Biblical Research* 26 (1991): 19–29.

White, L. Michael. "Urban Development and Social Change in Imperial Ephesos." Pages 27–65 in *Ephesos: Metropolis of Asia.* Ed. Helmut Koester. Valley Forge, Penn.: Trinity Press International, 1995.

Wild, R. A. "The Known Isis-Serapis Sanctuaries from the Roman Period." *ANRW* 17.4:1739–1851. Part 2, *Principat,* 17.4. Ed. H. Temporini and W. Haase. New York: de Gruyter, 1989.

Wimmer, Joseph F. *Fasting in the New Testament*. New York: Paulist, 1982.

Winston, David. *The Wisdom of Solomon*. AB 43. New York: Doubleday, 1979.

Wiseman, D. J. "A New Text of the Babylonian Poem of the Righteous Sufferer." *Anatolian Studies* 30 (1980): 101–7.

Witt, R. E. *Isis in the Ancient World*. Baltimore: Johns Hopkins University Press, 1997.

Wright, N. T. *The New Testament and the People of God*. Minneapolis: Fortress, 1992.

Yadin, Yigael. מגלת המקדש. 2 vols. Jerusalem: The Israel Exploration Society and the Shrine of the Book, 1977.

Yardeni, Ada. "Breaking the Missing Link." *Biblical Archeology Review* 24 (3, 1998): 44–47.

_____. "A Draft of a Deed of an Ostracon from Khirbet Qumran." *Israel Exploration Journal* 47 (3–4, 1997): 233–37.

Yong-Eui, Yang. *Jesus and the Sabbath in Matthew's Gospel*. Sheffield: Sheffield Academic Press, 1997.

Zias, Joseph. "Death and Disease in Ancient Israel." *Biblical Archaeologist* 54 (3, 1991): 146–59.

Zias, Joseph, and K. Numeroff. "Ancient Dentistry in the Eastern Mediterranean: A Brief Overview." *Israel Exploration Journal* 36 (1986): 65–67.

Index of Subjects

Index of Modern Authors

Index of Ancient Sources

Gospel of Thomas
14.2   104

Ignatius

To the Ephesians
7.2   136

Irenaeus

Against Heresies
94
22.4   138

Justin Martyr

Second Apology
6   136

Origen

Against Celsus
84, 137

Tatian

Oratio ad Graecos
18   136

Tertullian
95

Apology
14.5   138
39.5   138

*Prescription against
    Heretics*
54

To Scapula
4   136

**Other Ancient
Writers**

Aelian
64, 92

Fragments
137

Nature of Animals
11:33   133

Apuleius
92

Metamorphoses
80, 101
5.10   136
11.19   139
11.28   138
11.30   137

Aristides
69

Oratio
39.1–18   134

Aristophanes

The Rich Man
112

Cato the elder
77

Celsus
78

De Medicina
56, 79, 81
2.33.6   136
3.21.2   136
5.22.4   135
6.6.8b   135
7.7.1   136
8.2.3–6   136
10.1   136

Dioscorides

De Materia Medica
78, 135

Galen
55, 78, 79, 92, 104,
124

On Physicians
77, 79
89   140
113   139

Hippocrates
55

Decorum
77

The Nature of Man
65
4   133

The Sacred Disease
56, 66, 132

Homer

Iliad
4.194   49

Josephus

Against Apion
1.281   133
1.282–283   133
1.284   133
1.288–292   134
1.295–311   134

Jewish Antiquities
17.169–176   100, 138

Jewish War
2.135   135

Life
104
403–404   135

Libanius
92

Declamationes
34.23–26   137
34.38–42   140

Oratio
30.39   139

Pausanias
101

Descriptio Graeciae
8.54.5   139
10.32.12   139

Philostratus

Apollonius of Tyana
93
7.39   138

Plato

Republic
36
3.406D   127
3.407E   127
3.408B   128

Pliny the Elder
92

Natural History
29.1   137
29.5.11   135
31.8.11   138
31.8.12   138

Plutarch
54, 93

Isis and Osiris
80   138

Porphyry
69

De abstinentia
2.19   134

Rufus of Ephesus
135

Seneca

On benefits
6.15.2   135

Strabo
102

Geographica
8.6.15   139
9.5.17   129

Suetonius
68

Claudius
25.2   134

Themistius
101

Oratio
27   139

Thucydides
2.47–55   130

Akkadian Texts

AMT
9.1:27–28   137

LABS
296, rev. lines
3–14   127
296, rev. lines
8–13   127

Ludlul bēl nēmeqi
37

RIME (Frayne)
E.4.1.7.2001, line
3   131
E.4.2.13.22, line
12   131

Greek Papyri

PGM
CXVII   1356

Testimonia of Asclepius
T. 318   134
T. 385   139
T. 421:641–643   140
T. 422   133
T. 455   137
T. 464b   137
T. 499   139
T. 539   137
T. 540   140
T. 714   129
T. 735   139
T. 772   139
T. 804   134
T. 817   139
T. 834   139

**Rabbinic and
Targumic Literature**

Mishna

ᶜ*Aboda Zara*
2.2.   78

Tosefta Hulin
22.23   134

Berakot (Jerusalem)
9.12 p. 13a   134

Targum Onqelos
42

Incantation Bowl

(Naveh and Shaked)
76